THE TECHNICAL ELITE

THE
TECHNICAL
ELITE

By
JAY M. GOULD

AUGUSTUS M. KELLEY · PUBLISHER
NEW YORK · 1966

LIBRARY OF CONGRESS CATALOGUE CARD NUMBER
66 - 15566

PRINTED IN THE UNITED STATES OF AMERICA
by SENTRY PRESS, NEW YORK, N. Y. 10019

98720

AUTHOR'S ACKNOWLEDGEMENTS

I had the opportunity to develop the ideas offered here in the course of preparing some statistical estimates of the magnitude and characteristics of the universe of scientists, engineers and technical managers from which the readers of the periodical *Scientific American* are drawn. Many of the statistics and charts used here were indeed first published by *Scientific American* in a series of brochures entitled: "U.S. Industry: Under New Management" (1963); "Subscriber Portrait No. 59" (1963); "How Industry Buys No. 2" (1964); and "The Big Business Executive/1964" (1965).

I am grateful to the publishers of *Scientific American* for permission to use these statistical materials, but they do not of course share any responsibility for the interpretation I have given them here. I must also acknowledge the encouragement of Augustus M. Kelley, whose recent republication of the collected works of Thorstein Veblen suggested the need for a reappraisal of Veblen in the light of the scientific revolution of our time, whose impact on industrial productivity Veblen was the first to appreciate. Although originally designed as an introduction to a new edition of Veblen's *The Engineers and the Price System* the present work assumed more ambitious proportions and is being offered as a separate

1

publication with the hope that it can help reawaken interest in the ideas of that long neglected giant of American economics.

I must make a final acknowledgement to the late Prof. Wesley C. Mitchell and to the National Bureau of Economic Research, where I first grappled with the statistical problem of accounting for gains in industrial productivity. I was lucky enough to fall under Prof. Mitchell's magic spell both at the National Bureau and at Columbia University, and had been struck by Mitchell's sympathetic treatment of Veblen in his famous course on the development of economic thought. I like to think that I also absorbed Mitchell's basic emphasis on the need for any economic theory to rest on a statistical framework, susceptible to objective measurement and test.

TABLE OF CONTENTS

LIST OF CHARTS

I INTRODUCTION

The accelerating advance of American technology
in the post-war era is profoundly affecting all aspects
of our economic, social and political life. Not of least
importance is the consequent emergence of a new
technical elite, whose influence on the higher levels
of decision-making in government and industry has
been dramatically celebrated, albeit in sharply con-
trasting ways, in the "two cultures" debate set off
by C. P. Snow and by President Eisenhower in his
famous valedictory warning of the danger that
"public policy could itself become the captive of a
scientific-technological elite." In this context, an
American "scientific establishment" has been defined
to include perhaps as few as 200 persons "who significantly and directly influence the availability of scientific knowledge and ideas and their application" or
as many as the one hundred thousand persons listed
in *American Men of Science.**

We are concerned here with a somewhat more
specific concept of the technical elite in industry—
that is, those persons with training in the natural
sciences or engineering who can be shown to be increasingly responsible for the enormous productivity
of American industrial enterprise. An elite status is

---

* R. Gilpin and C. Wright, *Scientists and National Policy Making* (New
York: Columbia University Press, 1964) pp. 47, 48.

7

conferred on this technical corps by virtue of its high degree of education and its above-average income. Furthermore, its three chief components are among the very few highly paid occupational categories now undergoing rapid expansion in America today.

Of these three basic occupational groups, the smallest in number, but most potent in terms of its long-range effect on productivity, are the natural scientists. Of a total of 325,000 natural scientists in the United States in 1965, about 125,000 are engaged in teaching and research in colleges and universities and the remaining 200,000 work in government, industry, and research laboratories.

The largest component of the technical elite—the engineers—number close to one million in the United States today, almost all of whom are in industry and government.

The third key component is technical management, by which we mean the salaried managers in industry who have had technical training (a college or higher degree in natural science or engineering) or those who, without such formal technical education, nevertheless discharge technical functions in production, design, or research and development.

At present there are about 325,000 such managers with salaries over $10,000 per year,.200,000 of whom are in manufacturing alone. Centering our attention on only those scientists, engineers, and technical managers in industry and government with annual salaries above $10,000, we can account for a technical elite of close to one million persons, of whom 500,000 are in manufacturing. As members of a technical labor force growing at an annual rate in excess of 5 percent, their numbers have doubled in the past decade. But even this is an inadequate measure of the degree to which the technical elite, by virtue of their even more explosive effects on the productivity of American industry, is helping to expand our potential and actual capacity to produce at levels that would seem Utopian to any earlier generation.

The vision of unparalleled abundance as the realizable goal of modern technology can be traced in the writings of several notable American social scientists, particularly Henry Adams and Thorstein Veblen. Conditioned by American historical experience, they placed far greater emphasis on the role of the scientist and technologist in the process of economic advance than did European historians and economists, who viewed the development of Western civilization primarily as a slow and painful accumulation of capital resources.

Adams and Veblen were also the first to see clearly some of the social and economic implications of the fact that the growth of science and technology was exponential in nature; which can be translated to mean—the bigger it gets, the more it grows.

Writing in 1909, Adams viewed the development of human thought as passing through successive stages of abstraction, with each phase spanning progressively shorter time intervals. Thus the 300-year period from 1600 to 1900, which he dubbed the "mechanical phase," had been preceded by a "religious phase" that had lasted for thousands of years. This in turn had been preceded by phases in which thought had gradually replaced instinct over time periods measured in millenia. In each phase there could be discerned a quickening in the development of thought. He wrote:

> The acceleration of the 17th century, as compared with that of any previous age, was rapid, and that of the 18th century was startling. The acceleration became even measurable, for it took the form of utilizing heat as force, through the steam engine, and this addition of power was measurable in the coal output. . .

> The world did not double or treble its movement between 1800 and 1900, but, measured by any standard known to science—by horsepower, calories, volts, mass in any shape—the tension and vibration and volume and so-called progression of society were fully a thousand times greater in 1900 than in 1800.

Looking ahead to the next phase, he foresaw that the future of Thought, and therefore of History, lies in the hands of the physicists.

In the coming phase, which, judging by the progressive temporal contraction of previous phases, he thought would come to an end perhaps as early as

1921 and probably no later than 2025, be predicted that

> Thought should continue to act as the universal solvent, which it is, and should reduce the forces of the molecule, the atom and the electron to that costless servitude to which it has reduced the old elements of earth and air, fire and water.*

This remarkably prophetic vision was shared by Thorstein Veblen, who regarded the rapidity with which modern technology was developing as a prime factor in his analysis of social and economic institutions. The prophetic power of this technological emphasis was dramatically revealed by Veblen's writings during World War I, namely, *Imperial Germany and the Industrial Revolution* (1915), *The Nature of Peace* (1919), and "The Opportunity of Japan" (1915).†

In these essays, Veblen foresaw that both Germany and Japan, where in each case an advanced modern technology had been grafted onto a semi-feudal social base held over from a "past predatory" era, must inevitably engage in wars of aggression. However, he also foresaw that the attempt to join two such radically conflicting traditions would be inherently anachronistic and unstable and, therefore, doomed to failure. But Veblen saw great technical

---

* Henry Adams, *The Degradation of the Democratic Dogma* (New York: Macmillan, 1919) p. 309.
† Reprinted in Thorstein Veblen, *Essays in Our Changing Order* (New York: The Viking Press, 1934).

advantages for Germany (and for Japan, too) in being comparative late-comers, for they needed only to borrow the most advanced techniques from a wide range of technologies and types of capital equipment, which of necessity included much that was already obsolescent.

In the post-war period following the defeat of these two predatory, dynastic states, Veblen also foresaw the need for

> the disestablishment of the Imperial Dynasty and the abrogation of all feudalistic remnants of privilege.

The defeated dynasties must be strictly disarmed for a long enough time to permit a peaceful outlook to be generated by the development of the discipline of modern machine technology. He implied that both countries, being possessors of modern technical "know-how," could rapidly undergo an industrial resurgence in the post-war period, particularly because capital equipment destroyed by the war could be replaced by newer and more efficient machinery. Without going into Veblen's analysis of the causes of the irreconcilable conflict between modern technology and the dynastic, semi-feudal traditions of Germany and Japan—which would take us too far afield—we can, however, take note of the extent to which Veblen's prevision has been vindicated by history in the intervening four decades.

But an even greater predictive value must be

credited to Veblen's analysis of the way in which modern technology would come into conflict with the business enterprise system in America and mold it to its own deep-seated and overriding requirements. This is the theme of Veblen's *The Engineers and the Price System,* an impassioned book written in 1919 in the excitement engendered by the ending of World War I and amid expectations of great impending change. Although the 'twenties did not seem to fulfill the perspectives invoked by *The Engineers and the Price System,* the book appeared to have a greater urgency during the depression-ridden 'thirties, when the engineer was represented by the Technocrats as the only potential, rational force that could salvage a disordered economy. But this book is even more directly addressed to our own time, when a new technical elite is finally emerging and is inducting American industry into the age of automation.

In this essay I have sought to interpret the perhaps startling measurements of the growth and magnitude of the technical elite in America today against the setting provided by Veblen's writings, particularly in *The Engineers and the Price System,* which offers what can be called a theory of a technical elite. Although some people regard *The Engineers and the Price System* as a call for revolution, others see the work as an elitist program of social action replacing the Marxist concept of the working class as the main agent of social and economic change. Veblen stated that the engineers constitute the indispensable General Staff of the industrial system. Their class consciousness has taken the immediate form of a growing sense of waste and confusion. . . . So the engineers are beginning to draw together and ask themselves, "What about it?"*

Edwin Layton has commented on the irony that the engineer of Veblen's time formed one of the most conservative groups in the nation, whose foremost spokesman was Herbert Hoover.†

But Veblen did not think that the engineer of his time would initiate programs for social change, nor could they

reach a common understanding . . . and agree on a plan for action . . . there is assuredly no present promise of the technician's turning their insight and common sense to such use. There need be no present apprehension. The technicians are a "safe and sane" lot, on the whole; and they are pretty well commercialized, particularly the older generation, who speak with authority and conviction, and to whom the younger generation of engineers defer, on the whole, with such a degree of filial piety as should go far to reassure all good citizens.‡

---

* Thorstein Veblen, *The Engineers and the Price System* (New York: B. W. Huebsch, 1921) p. 71.
† Edwin Layton, "Veblen and the Engineers," *American Quarterly*, XIV (Spring 1962).
‡ Veblen, *op. cit.*, p. 137.

A literal acceptance of the engineer as a pivotal agent of change misses the real point that Veblen was making here: namely, that technology—the joint creation of the artisan, the technician, the engineer, and, later, the scientist, all brought together by the captains of industry and of finance—has an inner logic and dynamism somewhat separate from that of the system of private enterprise of the West under which the technology evolved. In this book we shall explore the relevance of this theme as it applies to the contemporary role of the technical elite in the organization and direction of American industry.

II THE LIMITATION OF OUTPUT

A duality that runs through all of Veblen's work is the contrast between the needs of modern industrial technology and those of the "pecuniary" or "business" system that developed in England and America over the past 200 years. In *The Engineers and the Price System,* this conflict is dramatized much more forcefully than ever before, for in this book Veblen eschewed the involved, oblique style that had puzzled many readers of the earlier *Theory of the Leisure Class* (1899) and the *Theory of Business Enterprise* (1904). Here Veblen drew his contrasts so starkly as almost to invite parody. At the one pole we have the noble forces of reason represented by the engineer, or the industrial expert or skilled technologist, who is charged with the responsibility of maintaining the delicate balance of an industrial system that

> runs on as an inclusive organization of many and diverse interlocking mechanical processes, interdependent and balanced among themselves in such a way that the due working of any part of it is conditioned on the due working of all the rest. Therefore it will work at its best only on condition that these industrial experts, production engineers, will work together on a common

17

understanding; and more particularly on condition that they must not work at cross purposes. These technological specialists whose constant supervision is indispensable to the due working of the industrial system constitute the general staff of industry, whose work it is to control the strategy of production at large and to keep an oversight of the tactics of production in detail.*

At the other pole we have the captains of finance who are described as practicing a rather sinister "conscientious withdrawal of efficiency" in order to maintain

prices at a profitable level by curtailment of output rather than by lowering production-cost per unit of output, because they have not had such a working acquaintance with the technological facts in the case as would enable them to form a passably sound judgment of suitable ways and means for lowering production-cost; and at the same time, being shrewd business men, they have been unable to rely on the hired-man's-loyalty of technologists whom they do not understand. The result has been a somewhat distrustful blindfold choice of processes and personnel and a consequent enforced incompetence in the management of industry, a curtailment of output below the needs of the community, below the produc-

---

* *The Engineers and the Price System*, pp. 52-53.

tive capacity of the industrial system, and below what an intelligent control of production would have made commercially profitable.*

Although Veblen used such euphemisms as "wastefulness" and "sabotage," his indictment of business rests here on grounds of relative inefficiency. Among the business practices that tend to negate the productive efforts of the engineer, Veblen included salesmanship, advertising, monopoly control, absentee ownership, financial speculation, and, in general, any failure of a market-oriented economy to achieve full capacity levels of output. It is easy to see in this critique the reasons for Veblen's popularity during the Great Depression. The hearings of the famous Temporary National Economic Committee in the late 'thirties, in which attention was focused on the precise quantitative measurement of unused capacity, could be regarded as official recognition of the validity of Veblen's analysis as applied to the inadequate functioning of the American economy of those years.

Veblen himself, however, had been sorely handicapped by the lack of statistics that his theories required both for confirmation and for precision. Subtleties and shadings having to do with degrees and magnitudes were frequently obscured by his sometimes heavy-handed search for the particularly trenchant phrase that would most wound the sensi-

---

* *The Engineers and the Price System*, p. 62.

bilities of believers in the "received" economic doctrines.*

We may note, for example, his rather hazy speculations on the degree to which capacity was limited by the business system. It makes a big difference, after all, if this percentage is of the order of 25, 50, or 75. That he leaned toward the middle figure is indicated by his statement that

> The eventual elimination of salesmanship and sales-cost would lighten the burden of workday production for the underlying population by some fifty percent.†

In *The Vested Interests and the Common Man* (written in 1918) he dealt with this point at somewhat greater length:

> The question as to how much this "incapacity by advisement" has commonly amounted to may be attempted somewhat after this fashion. Today, under compulsion of patriotic devotion, fear, shame and bitter need, and under the un-

---

* The American economist who was perhaps most profoundly affected by Veblen was Wesley C. Mitchell. Although he absorbed much of Veblen's skepticism about "received" economic theories, he set himself the task of elaborating the quantitative measures that could put such theories to the test. Mitchell founded the National Bureau of Economic Research at about this time, which has since developed the important statistical measures of business cycle fluctuation, national income, and productivity. The Brookings Institute also embarked on a similar program and in the 'twenties addressed itself to measures of capacity.

† *The Engineers and the Price System*, p. 113.

precedentedly shrewd surveillance of public
officers bent on maximum production, the great
essential industries controlled by the vested
interests may, one with another, be considered
to approach—perhaps even conceivable to exceed
—a fifty-percent efficiency; as counted on the
basis of what should ordinarily be accomplished
by use of an equally costly equipment having
the disposal of an equally large and efficient labor
force and equally good natural resources, in case
the organization were designed and managed
with an eye single to turning out a serviceable
product, instead of, as usual, being managed with
an eye single to private gain in terms of price.

To the spokesmen of "business as usual" this
rating of current production under the pressure
of war needs may seem extravagantly low;
whereas, to the experts in industrial engineering,
who are in the habit of arguing in terms of material cost and mechanical output, it will seem
extravagantly high. Publicly, and concessively,
this latter class will speak of a 25 percent efficiency; in private and confidentially they appear
disposed to say that the rating should be nearer
to 10 percent than 25. To avoid any appearance
of an ungenerous bias, then, present actual production in these essential industries may be
placed at something approaching 50 percent of
what should be their normal productive capacity
in the absence of a businesslike control looking

to "reasonable profits." It is necessary at this point to call to mind that the state of the industrial arts under the new order is highly productive,—beyond example.*

Veblen's concept of maximum "efficiency" advanced here is a technological one. It is the measure of maximum utilization of the capacity of a plant that an engineer would make on the assumption that the plant would run throughout the year without allowance for cyclical or seasonal variations in the demand for the output of the plant and allowing for only such interruptions as are necessary for proper maintenance of plant and equipment. Such a measure is perhaps particularly useful in wartime, when the demand for the output of the national economy is set at maximum levels with relatively little consideration for market demand fluctuations. In this sense, Veblen's speculation that only half of our industrial capacity would normally be in use was borne out by our performance in World War II, when in the period 1941-1943, industrial output more than doubled despite the mobilization into the armed forces of 11 million men.

But in peacetime, Veblen's technological concept of maximum capacity makes little sense to the practical economist, plant manager, or businessman who must live in a world of supply and demand, where

---

* *The Vested Interests and the Common Man* (New York: B. W. Hueback, 1919) p. 79.

plant output must be geared to such demand as can be met at a profit. Most statistical measures of capacity therefore make some assumptions as to what can be considered "normal" fluctuations in seasonal and cyclical demand. Thus the Brookings Institute estimated that a "practical"—as opposed to a theoretical or completely technological—measure of unused capacity of American industry in 1929 was of the order of 20% based on the "prevailing" customs as to the number of shifts, length of working day, and seasonal pattern. Similar measures were made in 1962 for the Joint Economic Committee by the McGraw Hill Department of Economics, which, based also on assumptions of "normal" working shifts and "normal" seasonal patterns, put the unused capacity of American industry in 1960 at 27%.*

But the difficulty with all such measures is how to decide what is "normal." After all, the auto industry frequently reaches an annual rate of production in the closing two or three months of the calendar year that is twice as great as total output for that year, but few economists would therefore rate the auto industry as subject to 50% under-utilization, for this is a "normal" seasonal pattern. There remains a vast gulf, then, between Veblen's technological measure of capacity and any measure which must make some allowance for the fluctuations of demand of a free market economy.

* "Measures of Productive Capacity," Report of the Subcommittee on Economic Statistics to the Joint Economic Committee, July 24, 1962.

23

Interest in the Veblenian concept of unused capacity tends to ebb in peak years and to revive in the trough years of the business cycle when the disparity between the capacity to produce and the cyclically restricted output levels becomes something that people feel intuitively even though the disparity may not be precisely measurable.

In the recent past, critics of the workings of the American economy have shifted emphasis away from the presumed wastes of advertising, salesmanship, and unused capacity. In an economy faced with the more important problem of finding jobs for increasing numbers displaced by machines, employment in advertising and in sales is eagerly welcomed, for such activities are seen as increasingly necessary to "move" the goods pouring out of a superlatively productive economy. So on this score Veblen's attack on the wastefulness of American business practice carries rather little weight today. And among the problems besetting an affluent society, those involved in increasing the efficiency of production may seem to some relatively remote.

A believer in the "received" economic doctrines could advance one argument with respect to utilization of capacity that would give Veblen pause: What could be more disruptive to the attempt to maintain full capacity operation than a new technological process that would render obsolete all old plants operating under the old technology? Without the free play of the market how can we judge whether a particular technology is obsolete? Is it not unfair for Veblen to scold the captain of industry for his alleged reluctance to introduce the disruptive effects of a new technical innovation and, at the same time, to berate him for limiting the utilization of capacity, since the innovation would itself generate much excess capacity? And, finally, is not the pursuit of profit, in a freely fluctuating market economy, responsible not only for the apparent but perhaps necessary wastes but also for the technical advances that have been so productive as to make inconsequential the wastefulness of the practices Veblen deplored? These questions go to the very heart of the relation between technology and economic advance and are more fundamental than the issue of unused capacity treated *in vacuo*.

Veblen's reply to these questions would begin typically with an historical review of the way in which modern technology was brought into being under the spur of the profit motive, animating the early captains of industry

> who made it their work to carry the industrial promise of the Revolution out into tangible performance, during the closing decades of the eighteenth and the early decades of the nineteenth century. These captains of the early time are likely to be rated as inventors, at least in a loose sense of the word. But it is more to the point that they were designers and builders of factory, mill, and mine equipment, of engines,

processes, machines, and machine tools, as well as shop managers, at the same time that they took care, more or less effectually, of the financial end. Nowhere do these beginnings of the captain of industry stand out so convincingly as among the English tool-builders of that early time, who designed, tried out, built, and marketed that series of indispensable machine tools that has made the practical foundation of the mechanical industry. Something to much the same effect is due to be said for the pioneering work of the Americans along the same general lines of mechanical design and performance at a slightly later period. To men of this class the new industrial order owes much of its early success as well as of its later growth.

These men were captains of industry, entrepreneurs, in some such simple and comprehensive sense of the word as that which the economists appear to have had in mind for a hundred years after, when they have spoken of the wages of management that are due the entrepreneur for productive work done. They were a cross between a businessman and an industrial expert, and the industrial expert appears to have been the more valuable half in their composition. But factory, mine, and ship owners, as well as merchants and bankers, also made up a vital part of that business community out of whose later growth and specialization the corporation financier of the nineteenth and twentieth centuries has arisen. His origins are both technological and commercial, and in that early phase of his life history which has been taken over into the traditions of economic theory and of common sense he carried on both of these lines of interest and of work in combination. That was before the large scale, the wide sweep, and the profound specialization of the advanced mechanical industry had gathered headway.*

In this early period of the development of the business enterprise system, profit was largely a measure of the productive efficiency of the technical innovation introduced by the captain of industry. The productive value of any given item of industrial equipment, which mirrors the technological component of profit

> is measured by its effective use of the technological knowledge current in the community for the time being.†

But along about the end of the nineteenth century the composition of profit began to mirror the change in the scale and complexity of modern corporate enterprise.

> But progressively the cares of business management grew larger and more exacting, as the scale of things in business grew larger, and so

---

* *The Engineers and the Price System*, pp. 32-34.
† *The Vested Interests and the Common Man*, p. 68.

the directive head of any such business concern came progressively to give his attention more and more exclusively to the "financial end." At the same time and driven by the same considerations the businesslike management of industry has progressively been shifting to the footing of corporation finance. This has brought on a further division, dividing the ownership of the industrial equipment and resources from their management. . . .

In point of time this critical period in the affairs of industrial business coincides roughly with the coming in of corporation finance as the ordinary and typical method of controlling the industrial output. Of course the corporation, or company, has other uses besides the restrictive control of the output with a view to a profitable market, but it should be sufficiently obvious that the combination of ownership and centralization of control which the corporation brings about is also exceedingly convenient for that purpose. And when it appears that the general resort to corporate organization of the larger sort sets in about the time when business exigencies begin to dictate an imperative restriction of output, it is not easy to avoid the conclusion that this was one of the ends to be served by this reorganization of business enterprise. Business enterprise may fairly be said to have shifted from the footing of free-swung competitive production to that of a "conscientious withholding of efficiency," so soon and so far as corporation finance on a sufficiently large scale had come to be the controlling factor in industry. At the same time and in the same degree the discretionary control of industry, and of other business enterprise in great part, has passed into the hands of the corporation financier.*

Profit must now also cover the "vested interest" of the corporate leaders of business and finance. Their income is the capitalized value of income not assignable to any specific material factor as its productive source and represents all the wastes involved in monopoly, restricted output, salesmanship, etc.:

> The business man's place in the economy of nature is to "make money," not to produce goods. The production of goods is a mechanical process, incidental to the making of money; whereas the making of money is a pecuniary operation, carried on by bargain and sale, not by mechanical appliances and powers. The business men make use of the mechanical appliances and powers of the industrial system, but they make a pecuniary use of them. And in point of fact the less use a business man can make of the mechanical appliances and powers under his charge, and the smaller a product he can contrive to turn out for a given return in terms of price, the better it suits his purpose. The highest achievement in

---

* *The Engineers and the Price System*, pp. 34, 37-38.

business is the nearest approach to getting something for nothing. What any given business concern gains must come out of the total output of productive industry, of course; and to that extent any given business concern has an interest in the continued production of goods. But the less any given business concern can contrive to give for what it gets, the more profitable its own traffic will be. Business success means "getting the best of the bargain."*

Thus Veblen is not really attacking the role of profits as such in the pecuniary system but rather the tendency for the latter day corporate leaders of business to maximize that portion of profit that is not representative of the contribution of technology. In fact their direction leads to output levels which are "below what an intelligent control of production would have made commercially profitable."†

Here, then, is the nub of Veblen's argument: An intelligent control (i.e., technological) of production would be even more profitable than that of the typical business interests, and such profits would be proportionately more beneficial to society.

Veblen believed firmly in the social utility of the profit motive as a spur to technical innovation. While he saw an unavoidable conflict between the business view of profit and that of science, he found no sub-

---

* The Vested Interests and the Common Man, p. 92.
† The Engineers and the Price System, p. 62.

stitute for the margin of profit, even subject as it was to the manipulation of business, as the basic reflector of the contribution of science and human creativity to economic advance.

In the perspective of the half century since Veblen first formulated his critique of the performance of American Big Business, we can now state that on the level of the efficient management of the individual enterprise, the gap between business and science has narrowed considerably. We can show that the management of American corporate enterprise can be increasingly termed scientific in two significant senses. First we can show that managerial functions are increasingly exercised by men with scientific and technical as well as business training. Secondly, successful business administration today involves management techniques which can be increasingly called "scientific," although the term can be easily misused. Modern business expertise includes the use of sophisticated principles of cost accounting, automatic data processing, inventory control, the optimum location of plant and warehouse facilities, traffic management, packaging, merchandising, marketing research and advertising. For each firm, business success rests, not only on technological innovation, but on the more or less intelligent application of these modern managerial techniques to the task of maximizing sales and the difference between receipts and costs.

A relatively small percentage of all technological innovations will be successful, so that an element of risk must attend the introduction of any new product or process. Profit remains the indispensable arbiter of whether or not something new has really been added. Finally as we shall show, the advent of the computer in business administration today makes it increasingly difficult to draw a meaningful line between the business and the technological component of profit.

Present-day critics of the presumed "wastefulness" of advertising must use criteria other than those advanced by Veblen. For the individual enterprise, advertising (despite difficulties in any precise evaluation of its effectiveness) remains a powerful mechanism to equate a given supply with an existing potential demand, and the intelligent use of advertising in "clearing the shelves" can make as great a contribution to the maximization of sales and profit, as the well-timed introduction of technological innovation.

Thus it can be said that American Big Business today has stolen much of Veblen's thunder. It can no longer be said that the "shrewd businessmen . . . are unable to rely on the hired-man's-loyalty of technologists whom they do not understand." The typical modern American corporation, in pursuit of private profit, is an extremely efficient engine for applying both advanced managerial techniques and new technology to the production and distribution of goods and services, even by Veblen's standards. But Veblen can be seen today as having won a quiet victory, in having foreseen the emergence of a technical elite to harness the divergent interests of business and science.

III THE EMERGENCE OF A TECHNICAL LABOR FORCE

The impact of Veblen's argument on the present-day American industrial system can be best appreciated by borrowing a leaf from Veblen's method and briefly sketching the historical development of American science and technology over the past two centuries, in terms of some key quantitative measures.

Historical estimates of the number of practising engineers and scientists in the United States add an element of precision to one's judgment of the accelerating pace of technical advance; such statistical measures were not available to Veblen, but the spirit of this chapter will be found in his writings, particularly in his essays on "The Place of Science in Modern Civilization" (1904)* and "The Technology of Chemistry and Physics" (1923).**

The census of 1920 reported the employment in industry of 172,000 engineers and chemists, comprising less than one-half of one percent of the 37 millions employed in all occupations in that year. This fact by itself might have raised questions as to why Veblen placed so great an emphasis on so tiny a

---

* Reprinted in *The Place of Science in Modern Civilization* (New York: B. W. Huebsch, 1919).

** *Absentee Ownership and Business Enterprise in Recent Times. The Case of America.* (New York: B. W. Huebsch, 1923) Chapter X.

segment of the labor force. The answer is twofold: not only is the function of the technologist in industry unique, but so explosive is the exponential growth rate of the technical work force in America that the 1920 figure represented the largest assemblage of industrial technologists in the world at that time.

It is an extraordinary fact that throughout our history the number of persons who could be considered fully engaged in technical pursuits has been growing at extremely high annual rates, running at levels between two and three times greater than the secular growth rates in population or production. This means that every generation in America, including our own, that of Veblen, and even that of the Founding Fathers, probably felt that it was living in a golden age of science and technology. In the words of de Solla Price, at any point in history

> One could look back and say that most of the scientists that have ever been are alive now, and most of what is known has been determined within recent memory.*

The writer has found that the historical growth in the total number of full-time scientists and engineers in the United States could be described by an exponential series that must have proceeded at an average annual rate of gain of 7 percent during the nineteenth

---

* Derek de Solla Price, *Little Science, Big Science* (New York: Columbia University Press, 1963) p. 14.

century in order to reach the level of 63,000 scientists and engineers recorded for 1900. This means that in this century the total number must have been roughly doubling every decade.

Growth rates in the eighteenth century were even higher, but this was the period when American technology began its development in response to the practical requirements of colonizing a New World. The concept that a person could be trained to pursue the technical arts evolved slowly and did not figure significantly at that time. It is instructive to analyze this early period, when a technical labor force first emerged in America.

Scientific interest in the period preceding the American Revolution was intense, as befitted a people dedicated to a belief in natural law and reason. Most of the nation's scientific figures could be found in the membership of the American Philosophical Society in Philadelphia, founded by Benjamin Franklin, and later in the American Academy of Arts and Sciences, established in Boston. But such membership also included leaders in the humanities, and few could be regarded as engaged solely in science or technology. In colonial times,

> Science was not separate from philosophy, the arts or literature in either organization or personnel. Within the framework of natural philosophy and natural history, the particular fields of physics and chemistry, botany, zoology and mineralogy were clear, but nobody imagined that a

man should devote his whole time to one of them. Indeed almost none of the members were professional scientists. Many were doctors, lawyers or clergymen making their living and spending much of their time in ways unconnected with science. Medicine provided perhaps the nearest approach to a scientific profession.*

Among the physicians there were many who made notable contributions to the study of botany and natural history.† But as Dr. Dupree has indicated, most of the members of the two societies were amateurs with sufficient economic means to sustain an interest in scientific study and speculation. There is a distinguished line of such amateurs in colonial times, starting perhaps with James Logan, a wealthy Quaker merchant credited with importing the first copy of Newton's *Principia Mathematica* into the New World and who, although self-taught, published a treatise on optics as early as 1739. Another notable example of the gentleman-scientist was Thomas Jefferson.

Nevertheless it is possible to single out the small number of men who can be considered to have been

---

* A. Hunter Dupree, *Science in the Federal Government* (Cambridge, Mass.: Harvard University Press, 1957) p. 7.

† For example, Cadwallader Colden, William Douglas, Alexander Garden, John Lining, Thomas Bond, and John Mitchell. All are listed in Brooke Hindle's excellent monograph, *The Pursuit of Science in Revolutionary America 1735-1789* (Chapel Hill: University of North Carolina Press, 1956).

fully engaged in the pursuit of scientific and technical knowledge in this period.

Foremost, of course, was Benjamin Franklin, whose experiments with electricity made him known to Europe as the New World's first and most distinguished scientist. John Bartram and David Rittenhouse must also be considered among the first full-time American scientists. Bartram was the first American botanist. Helped by contributions from wealthy patrons (including Logan and Franklin), he traveled throughout the colonies collecting seeds for his patrons and, in the course of such travels, published the earliest systematic studies of New World flora.

The need for surveyors in colonial times gave rise to a distinguished group of men interested in mathematical and geographic measurements. David Rittenhouse, a self-taught clockmaker and surveyor and a disciple of Franklin, invented a remarkably precise mechanical "orrery," or planetarium, which contributed greatly to early studies of astronomy in the colonies. Both Cadwallader Colden and James Alexander, as Surveyors-General of New York and New Jersey respectively, took advantage of their positions to pursue botanical and scientific interests. Other notable surveyors of the time interested in astronomical observation were John Leeds, William Parsons, and William Alexander.

Finally, there were the professors of "mathematics and natural philosophy" at the various colonial colleges. The most eminent was John Winthrop of Harvard, whose publications on astronomy were highly regarded. Others were the Rev. Thomas Clap (Yale), David Howell (Rhode Island), David Treadwell (King's College), William Small (William and Mary), Theophilus Grew (Philadelphia), Ezra Stiles (Yale), and, of course, Benjamin Rush, who became the first professor of chemistry in America at Philadelphia College in 1770, and James Smith, professor of chemistry at King's College, later succeeded by Peter Middleton.

Thus it is possible to estimate that at the time of the American Revolution there were between one and two dozen men who may be considered to have been fully engaged in technological and scientific pursuits. In point of fact, our exponential growth series can be projected further back in time so as to begin in the years between 1740 and 1750, when one could say that the first full-time technical man made his appearance on the scene. Dr. Hindle singles out 1743 as the year in which "Benjamin Franklin gave voice to exalted aspirations for American achievement in science. Franklin wrote in that year, Hindle quotes,

The first drudgery of settling new colonies which confines the attention of people to mere necessaries is now pretty well over; and there are many in every province in circumstances that set them at ease, and afford leisure to cultivate the finer arts and improve the common stock of knowledge.

Hindle then observes:

This was almost the first moment at which it would have been reasonable to think in terms of the intercolonial promotion of science as ties developed drawing the colonists in closer relationship not only with Englishmen but other Americans.*

If one were to personify the first full-time American scientist, the choice would probably fall between Benjamin Franklin, who withdrew from the printing trade in 1748 to devote the bulk of his vast energies to his educational and scientific interests, and John Bartram, whose botanical studies preceded Franklin's scientific work in point of time.

We have traced our series representing the technical work force in America to its very beginnings in order to dramatize the extraordinary power of its exponential growth—i.e., its capacity to double every decade—which has continued to our own time. As we shall see, an exponential growth rate of such magnitude, which has continued well into the twentieth century, must eventually create technical manpower reserves of such proportions as to affect radically the organization of industry and its direction.

That Veblen had some sense of this exponential growth rate is clear from the following:

The number and interplay of technological factors engaged in any major operation in industry

---

* Hindle, *op. cit.*, p. 1.

today are related to the corresponding facts of the middle nineteenth century somewhat as the mathematical cube is related to the square; and the increase and multiplication of these technological factors is going forward incontinently, at a constantly accelerated rate.*

But perhaps an even more notable fact that emerges from a historical study of technology is the increasing degree to which the trained scientist has contributed to its advance.

The detailed history of the steam engine, the railroad, the textile mill, the iron ship, could be written without more than passing reference to the scientific work of the period. For these devices were made possible largely by the method of empirical practice, by trial and selection; many lives were lost by the explosion of steam-boilers before the safety-valve was generally adopted. And although all these inventions would have been the better for science, they came into existence, for the most part, without its direct aid. It was the practical men in the mines, the factories, the machine shops and the clockmakers' shops and the locksmiths' shops or the curious amateurs with a turn for manipulating materials and imagining new processes who made them possible.†

---

* *Absentee Ownership,* p. 271.
† Lewis Mumford, *Technics and Civilization* (New York: Harcourt, Brace, 1934) p. 215.

But the "practical" task of creating a transportation and communications system to bind a new continent together quickly revealed the need for trained engineers in the early years of the nineteenth century. In 1825, in the wake of the construction of the Erie Canal, the first engineering school was established at Rensselaer under Amos Eaton. Eaton had studied under Benjamin Stillman, the first professor of chemistry at Yale, who in turn had been a student of Robert Hare at Pennsylvania in a line of succession going back to Benjamin Rush. Special technical schools were organized at Yale and Harvard in 1846, to be followed by the Massachusetts Institute of Technology in 1861, the Columbia School of Mines in 1864, and the Worcester Polytechnic Institute in 1868. In these schools it is easy to see in the student-teacher relationship the basis for exponential growth: By the turn of the century, M.I.T. had graduated 2000 men. At that time the roster of distinguished scientists trained in America included the names of Joseph Henry, William Bond, Josiah Gibbs, Henry Rowland, Edward Pickering, and Albert Michelson.

Even the work of the great American inventors of the nineteenth century, when set in chronological order, suggests the increasing extent to which trial-and-error experimentation was replaced by the systematic application of newly discovered scientific principles: Fulton, Whitney, Morse, Goodyear, Ericsson, McCormick, Howe, Singer, Deere, Kelly, Field,

Pullman, Remington, Westinghouse, Eastman, Bell, and Edison.

With Edison we have the emergence of the first large industrial research laboratory engaged in "planned" invention, so characteristic of present-day research and development. There can be no doubt that the increasingly prominent role of the scientist adds incalculably to the pace of technical advance, but the establishment of industrial laboratories came later, after the skepticism of the practical captains of industry had been overcome.

Samuel Dana may have been the first consulting chemist; in his work for the Merrimack Manufacturing Company from 1834 to 1868 he greatly advanced the technology of textile manufacturing. In 1863 the first chemical laboratory was established at Wyandotte, Michigan, to study the control of raw materials in making steel, and very soon after that chemists were employed to analyze the relative richness of iron ore.

In his autobiography, Andrew Carnegie described the change in the fortunes of Kloman, Carnegie and Co., after hiring a German chemist, Dr. Fricke, to analyze the content of iron ores:

> great secrets did the doctor open up to us. Iron stone from mines that had a great reputation was now found to contain ten, fifteen, and even twenty per cent less iron than it had been credited with. Mines that hitherto had a poor reputation we found to be yielding superior ore; the good

was bad and the bad was good, and everything was topsy-turvy. Nine-tenths of all the uncertainties of pig-iron making were dispelled under the burning sun of chemical knowledge.*

Professor Stillman, the younger, who succeeded his father at Yale, performed the first distillations of crude petroleum in 1859, which launched the oil refining industry. In 1886 the first chemist (H. B. Schmidt) was employed in the meat packing industry.†

By 1900 some 8800 professional chemists were employed in all branches of government and industry, particularly in copper refining, paper and pulp, corn products, photographic supplies, as well as the newly burgeoning chemical industry—all in all about ten times as many as were engaged in teaching.

Veblen characterized this period as follows:

In the third quarter of the century chemical science also began to take effect as a material factor in technology, and about the same time electrical science rose into consequence as an industrial force. Chemical processes had of course had their part in the industrial arts before that date, but it had on the whole been a matter of chemical rule-of-thumb rather than of chemical science, of general information and common no-

---

* Carnegie, Andrew. *Autobiography* (Boston: Houghton Mifflin Co., 1920) p. 182.
† Howard R. Bartlett, *The Development of Industrial Research in the U. S.*, National Resources Planning Board, Washington, D. C., 1940.

toriety rather than exact and calculable processes worked out by detailed experiment and computation in the chemical laboratories. Neither the industrial chemist nor the industrial laboratory had been counted in among the ways and means of production.

Metallurgy, e.g., as well as much of the work in dyeing, tanning, baking, brewing, and the like, have always been of the nature of chemical industry; but it was not until the middle of the nineteenth century and after that these things began to bulk large in the industrial arts and then fell into the hands of the chemical technicians and took their place in the technological scheme as recondite matters of applied science.*

By the turn of the century, the technical work force in America was composed of 45,000 engineers, 10,000 chemists, and about 8000 other natural scientists. Without having such estimates, Veblen had already sensed how explosive would be the impact of the pure research scientist (as opposed to the engineer) on technical development, and in 1904 he wrote,

In so far as touches the aims and the animus of scientific inquiry, as seen from the point of view of the scientist, it is a wholly fortuitous and insubstantial coincidence that much of the knowledge gained under machine-made canons of research can be turned to practical account.

---

* *Absentee Ownership*, p. 258.

Much of this knowledge is useful, or may be made so, by applying it to the control of the processes in which natural forces are engaged. This employment of scientific knowledge for useful ends is technology, in the broad sense in which the term includes, besides the machine industry proper, such branches of practice as engineering, agriculture, medicine, sanitation, and economic reforms. The reason why scientific theories can be turned to account for these practical ends is not that these ends are included in the scope of scientific inquiry . . .

But the canons of validity under whose guidance he works are those imposed by the modern technology, through habituation to its requirements; and therefore his results are available for the technological purpose. His canons of validity are made for him by the cultural situation; they are habits of thought imposed on him by the scheme of life current in the community in which he lives; and under modern conditions this scheme of life is largely machine-made. In the modern culture, industry, industrial processes, and industrial products have progressively gained upon humanity, until these creations of man's ingenuity have latterly come to take the dominant place in the cultural scheme; and it is not too much to say that they have become the chief force in shaping men's daily life, and therefore the chief factor in shaping men's habits of

45

thought. Hence men have learned to think in the terms in which the technological processes act. This is particularly true of those men who by virtue of a peculiarly strong susceptibility in this direction become addicted to that habit of matter-of-fact inquiry that constitutes scientific research.*

* *The Place of Science in Modern Civilization*, p. 17.

IV THE TECHNICAL LABOR FORCE IN THE 20TH CENTURY

Veblen was so deeply impressed by the great technological achievements of his time that he took an indulgent view of the relatively primitive technology of the nineteenth century:

But taken as a whole and seen in the perspective of the twentieth century the mechanical industry of that time looks like a technological province. Industrial electricity and industrial chemistry had virtually no place in that scheme of things. There was no petroleum, virtually no industrial use of rubber, and virtually no use of cement. These things were not precisely unknown, but they were things which it was not then quite necessary to know anything about. The working scheme of things got along well enough without them. Refrigeration was still unknown, industrially; the hermetically sealed tin had not become a part of daily life; and the internal-combustion engine had not been invented, not even the rudimentary Otto gas-engine.*

An even wider gulf separates the technology of our time from that of Veblen's, but the basic pattern of future change was clearly visible to Veblen. The con-

---

* *Absentee Ownership*, p. 265.

tinued exponential growth in the technical labor force has brought the total number of scientists and engineers in the United States to 1.4 million in 1965, and government agencies predict that by 1970 nearly one out of every 20 members of the labor force will be an engineer, a scientist, a technician, or a teacher of technology.*

In addition, an examination of the changing composition of the technical work-force in the twentieth century reveals well-above-average growth rates in the new fields, a fact that bespeaks a growing sophistication in the scientific base of modern technology.

In order to assess the consistency and composition of the annual growth rate in science, the writer has assembled and examined data on the numbers of persons reporting themselves in decennial censuses as natural scientists and engineers. In addition, corresponding data collected in recent years by the National Science Foundation have been extrapolated back to 1900 on the basis of the available historical records of membership in the various technical societies in the United States. The consolidation of these independent series of data (Chart 2, p. 123) trace, with some reliability, the rise in the total number of natural scientists and engineers since 1900.

Between 1900 and 1960, the number increased from 63,000 to 1.2 million. This is equivalent to an

---

* "Profiles of Manpower in Science and Technology," National Science Foundation, Washington, D. C., 1953, p. 7.

annual gain of 5%. All branches of science and engineering exhibit annual growth rates of comparable magnitude. The number of physicists multiplied most rapidly at an annual growth rate of 7.5%; the number of chemists multiplied nearly elevenfold, equivalent to an annual growth rate of 4%.

While the aggregate numbers of scientists and engineers reported by the census from decade to decade may be regarded as reliable, the growth rates in particular fields cannot be taken too literally, because they are predicated upon less certain evidence and the numbers, field by field, are so small at the beginning of each series. The gain in the number of physicists, for example, from an estimated 400 in 1900 to 29,900 in 1960,* is based mainly on the increase in membership in the five societies comprising the American Institute of Physics, which grew from 96 in 1900 to 27,000 in 1960. (Separate calculations for the number of physicists engaged in college and university teaching showed a gain from 340 in 1900 to 8700 in 1960.) Despite the unavoidable error encountered when working with such small numbers in the early years, certain generalizations can be made about the comparative growth rates of the various fields.

Since 1900, the growth rate of the older and more numerous fields of "engineering" and "chemistry," which can be traced back to the decennial census of

* The figure for 1960 was estimated by the National Science Foundation.

1870, has proceeded at a more sedate pace than the "newer" and less populous scientific disciplines, which were first enumerated separately in the 1950 census. Thus, the number of engineers and chemists has increased at the rate of 4.8% per year while the total number of physicists, mathematicians, statisticians, actuaries, biologists, earth, agricultural and medical scientists has grown from about 8000 in 1900 to 247,000 in 1960, at an annual growth rate of 5.8%.

The curves that can be traced with reliability from 1900 onward, however, show a still more significant trend. In every technical field for which it is possible to compile decennial bench mark estimates, the growth rates in the period from 1930 to 1960 fall short of those registered in the period from 1900 to 1930, except for mathematics. Thus, growth in the total number of scientists and engineers, which proceeded at a 5.9% annual rate in the first three decades, dropped to 4.1% in the 1930-1960 period. The growth in the number of physicists, if we can accept the membership records of the American Institute of Physics as indicative, proceeded at an 8.1% annual rate in the 1900-1930 period and dropped to 6.9% in the succeeding three decades. The growth rate in the number of chemists, which rests on the more dependable census base, dropped from 5.6% in 1900-1930 to 2.5% in 1930-1960.* Indeed, in the final 1950-1960

---

* This is supported by membership records of the American Chemical Society, which increased more than twice as fast in the 1900-1930 period as in the 1930-1960 period.

decade, the number of chemists increased at a 1.5% annual rate, barely equal to the corresponding gain in population. Thus, it seems clear that retardation has characterized the later stages of growth in the various scientific disciplines in the United States.

Chart 2 summarizes the annual growth rates registered in each scientific field at decade intervals since 1930, when the evidence as to numbers in particular fields permits many reliable comparisons. The depression decade, 1930-1940, for example, clearly had an adverse effect on growth rates in all fields. However, the losses of potential candidates who could not afford to pursue their studies in the 'thirties, appear to have been offset in the two succeeding decades, when overall growth rates increased over those of the 'thirties. This fact has probably obscured the presence of retardation in the growth rates, which emerges only in tracing the long-term trends.

Some interesting divergent growth rates are reflected in Chart 2. Note, for example, the effect of the atomic research and development program on the acceleration of growth in the number of physicists in the 'forties and 'fifties. Such acceleration may have been at the expense of the related field of chemistry. Note, too, the extraordinary expansion in mathematics in the most recent period, reflecting the huge demand for programmers and computer systems analysts, for whom mathematics training is a major requirement. Biology, too, exhibits an accelerating growth rate in the most recent period. These divergent

51

growth rates would appear to reflect the lure of a scientific field, or subfield, in the exciting "breakthrough" period when new areas of research or development open up, as is now happening in the fields of molecular biology and computer technology. It appears, however, that the gains in these fields must be balanced by lags in the other, "older" fields.

Thornton Fry has given us a dramatic picture of the rapid development of a new technical field in its early stages.* In his many years of service at Bell Telephone Laboratories, Dr. Fry was in a position to observe the growth of a new scientific discipline (industrial mathematics) from almost its literal inception. He begins his statistical series with the hiring of Charles P. Steinmetz in 1888 by the forerunner of the General Electric Company as the first recorded instance of the employment of a mathematician in industry. By 1913, Dr. Fry estimated, there were about a dozen industrial mathematicians in the United States, mainly involved in the study of the mathematics of the transmission and generation of electric power and also in telephone transmission. By 1939 there were at least 150 members of the American Mathematical Society who "clearly had industrial or government employment."

Dr. Fry notes that these three bench-mark estimates trace an exponential growth curve with an annual rate of gain of about 11%. Extrapolated to

* T. C. Fry, "Mathematics in Industry—The First 75 years," *Science,* vol. 143 (1963), p. 934.

1963, the curve yields an estimate of 1800 industrial mathematicians, a number that coincides with Dr. Fry's independent head count of the number of qualified mathematicians with nonacademic employment in that year. Such consistency over a 75-year period tempted Dr. Fry to project continued gains at the same rate to the year 2013, when presumably 270,000 mathematicians might have nonacademic employment. He comments:

> I do not offer this as serious prophecy. . . . [The figures] do serve to indicate, however, the tremendous thrust of the social forces which have been injecting mathematicians in large numbers into industrial and government laboratories, an environment which only a few generations ago would have been judged inhospitable.*

As Dr. Fry's wry disclaimer suggests, annual growth rates of such magnitude must in the nature of things be subject to retardation. A systematic pattern of retardation has been found to characterize the secular growth pattern of individual industries.† In the absence of retardation, exponential growth rates must sooner rather than later generate magnitudes on the Munchausen scale.

If the totality of all scientists and engineers were to maintain a 5% annual gain for four more decades, for example, these professions would engage 9 million

---

* *Ibid.,* p. 935.
† Cf. Arthur F. Burns, *Production Trends in the U. S. Since 1870* (New York: National Bureau of Economic Research, 1934).

people by the year 2000. This would represent more than 6% of the total labor force projected for that year. But it is estimated that the top 6% of any age group have Army General Classification Test intelligence scores of 130 and above, which is the AGCT level associated with the ability to pursue graduate study.

Thus, a continued 5% annual growth in the technical component of the labor force would eventually require a complete draft of all persons of above-average intelligence without allowance for the arts, medicine, the social sciences, or other important fields of professional endeavor. Even if the pool of talent were to be doubled by lowering the barriers of discrimination against women and further expanded by opening the channels of opportunity to nonwhites and others now culturally deprived, the 9 million figure would constitute an exhorbitant claim upon the available capacity of society.

One could make a fairly simple assumption about the degree of retardation in the exponential growth pattern that would generate a series representing the total number of scientists and engineers in the United States for a period as long as three centuries. It accords with the statistical data on hand and involves no statistical extravagance for more than another 100 years to come. Such a series would begin with one in the year 1748, when Benjamin Franklin may be assumed to have represented the first full-time technologist, and, with an initial annual rate increase of 9%, would be subject to a 2.5% rate of retardation every 30 years.*

It is evident from Chart 1 that the decennial estimates of the "actual" numbers of scientists and engineers in the period 1900-1960 coincide closely with the "theoretical" estimates yielded by this assumption of slight but growing retardation. But such an assumption can rest on other grounds too. It must be conceded, for example, that gifted students are no longer being attracted to the sciences at the high rates observed in the 'fifties. This finding comes from a recent study of the careers and fields selected since 1957 by National Merit Scholarship Award semi-finalists upon graduation from high school, a group representing the top one percentile in scholastic aptitude.†

The study concentrated on both the "careers" and the major fields elected before and after entering college. Careers that have generally increased in popularity are (for boys) teaching, architecture, law, and medicine, and (for girls) law and government service. With respect to major fields, biology, history and mathematics are increasingly popular, while business, physics, engineering, and journalism are declining in

---

* The mathematical expression for such a function is $y = Ka^x b^{x^2/2} c^{x^3/6}$. In its logarithmic form, log c is the third derivative of log y with respect to the time variable χ and measures the constant rate of change (in this case, 2.5% every 30 years, or .08% per year) in the rate at which the annual growth rates are declining. The values of y generated by this function are plotted in Chart 1, p. 121.

† Robert C. Nichols, "Career Decisions of Very Able Students," *Science*, June 12, 1964, p. 1315.

popularity. The steepest decline was noted for chemical engineering, a net loss of about 45% in five years. The growing interest in biology and mathematics, running against a general decline of interest in scientific and engineering disciplines, would suggest again the lure of these "newer" fields. But more importantly, the study of the National Merit Scholars supports the conclusion that it would be wise to reckon with some over-all retardation in the growth of the numbers of able persons attracted to science and technology.

Such retardation would help to explain the small but persistent deficits that crop up in recent studies attempting to predict future demand and supply of technical personnel.* Both the National Planning Board and the National Science Foundation foresee a "demand" for 2.2 million scientists and engineers in 1970, based on projections of current rates of gain in industries increasingly requiring technical workers. But even with the optimistic assumption that colleges will be able to grant twice as many science degrees in 1970 as in 1960, the maximum "supply" projected for 1970 is 1.9 million scientists and engineers, a figure equivalent to an annual gain of 5.2% over 1960. If the pattern of retardation exhibited by the series shown in Chart 2 is accepted as a guide for the future, however, even the 1.9 million figure is too high. If

---

* *Scientists, Engineers and Technicians in the 1960's,* National Science Foundation, NSF 63-64, 1962; *Toward Better Utilization of Scientific and Engineering Talent,* Publication #1191, National Academy of Sciences, 1964.

annual growth rates on the order of 3.6% are to be expected during the 'sixties, as is suggested by this review of the long-term statistical trends, we shall have "only" 1.7 million scientists and engineers in 1970.

Given continued retardation in the rate of growth, it might be thought that simple extrapolation of the established trends would set the date when further growth will cease. Our growth model suggests, however, that such a point will not be reached even in the 21st century. By the year 2000, in fact, it forecasts a technical labor force of perhaps 3.5 million persons.

No tears need be shed over a failure to maintain a 5% exponential growth rate. A "scientific explosion" proceeding at an annual rate of 3 to 4 percent (implicit in our series for the remainder of the century) should generate enough forces to cope with the effects of the "population explosion," which in contrast is proceeding at the relatively moderate rate of less than 2 percent per year.

Exponential growth of the technical work-force has therefore not only continued in the twentieth century; its productivity has expanded by the broadening of its scientific base. But what is most notable is the degree to which American industry has in this century welcomed the contribution of the scientist and engineer to technology. The industrial research laboratory, which first emerged at the close of the nineteenth century and in which less than 8000 persons were employed in 1920,* today employs close to one million professionals, representing a growth rate of the order of 10% per year.

* Yale Bozen, "Trends in Industrial Research and Development," *Journal of Business,* July, 1960.

V THE TECHNICAL ELITE
IN INDUSTRY TODAY

The absorption of scientists and engineers into industry has proceeded in the past two decades at rates even higher than those governing the growth in their total number. This is a reflection of the great emphasis given to the postwar research and development boom. In addition to the demands generated by national defense considerations, the profitability and viability of business today is increasingly recognized as dependent on the march of new products and processes out of the thousands of research and development laboratories, large and small.

Whereas the indirect contribution of science to the productivity of industry has long been recognized, it was only in the 'fifties that the industrial employment of scientists, engineers, and their technical adjuncts—the technical managers and technicians—became large enough to permit precise measurement of their great direct contribution to industrial productivity.

In the period 1947-1961, total industrial output in the United States doubled, while total industrial employment remained unchanged. The consequent doubling in the productivity ratio is clearly associated with the accompanying doubling of the number of scientists and engineers employed in industry. (See Charts 4, 5 and 6, pp. 127-131.) But those industries with the highest ratios of technical employment registered gains in value-added per employee far greater than that of all other industries.*

The correlation between the gain in value-added per man and the technical employment ratio is seen to be quite systematic. At one end of the scale the chemicals industry, with the highest concentration of technical personnel (17%) registered the greatest productivity gain (143%). At the other extreme, the apparel industry, with a technical employment ratio of only 3%, increased its productivity by a mere 35%. Almost all the industries, when ranged from high to low in the order of technical ratios, manifest a corresponding decline in productivity gains.

This relationship cannot be the result of chance, though it may not be a causal one in the sense that the engagement of scientists and engineers would necessarily result in immediate increases in productivity; many other factors may be involved, such as the volume of capital investment, the average size of

---

* Census data are available to permit the calculation, for each of 20 basic manufacturing industries, of a technical employment ratio, which is defined as the ratio of employment of scientists, engineers, technicians, and salaried managers to total employment. This ratio averaged about 13% in 1960 for the "high-technology" industries taken together: chemicals, instruments, petroleum refining, electrical and non-electrical machinery, transportation equipment, and fabricated metals. For all other manufacturing industries, including rubber, stone, clay and glass, paper, food and other consumer goods, the average ratio of technical employment was 5%. High-technology industries increased their value-added-per-man ratios by 116% in the 1947-1961 period as against 88% for low-technology industries. See Charts 11, 12 and 13, pp. 141-145.

firm, and the degree of industry concentration or monopoly. Nevertheless we have here a dramatic illustration of the way in which the direct employment of technical people in industry is associated with greater efficiency of production and, therefore, with profitability.

Even the productivity gain of industries with very low technical employment ratios could be associated with science to the degree that they could buy their technology from other industries. Thus, the tobacco industry, which employs relatively few technical people, achieved large gains in productivity on the basis of highly automated equipment purchased from the industrial machinery industry.* Yet it appears that the direct employment of scientists and engineers in industry offers the prospect of additional gains in productivity, and therefore profitability, over and above the gains resulting from the purchase of technology from others.

---

* Another good example is American farming, which employs few scientists or technologists on the farm, but benefits greatly from the contributions to farm productivity of about 40,000 agricultural scientists employed mainly in government, colleges, experimental stations and by manufacturers of farm equipment, fertilizers, insecticides and pesticides. Consider too the printing and publishing industry, which in the past has been dominated by small shops, with little expenditure on research and development within the industry. This industry too will in the coming years experience a rapid rate of "technicalization" and consequent reorganization and productivity increase as the computer begins to automate the labor-intensive typesetting process. Even in the period 1958-1963 the productivity gain in printing and publishing was not too far behind the gain for all manufacturing. (See Chart 13, p. 145.)

Consequently, industry's search for talented men with scientific and technical skills has wrought a radical change in the income and status levels of such men over the past decade.

Dr. Herman Miller, of the United States Bureau of the Census, has published some startling figures pointing to so radical an alteration in the composition of top income earners since 1950 as to merit being termed an "income revolution," though not in the sense usually given to this overworked phrase. Dr. Miller's definition of the top 5% of income earners include those household heads who in 1960 enjoyed, from all sources, family incomes of more than $15,000. As dramatic evidence of the upgrading of income enjoyed by the typical affluent American family over that decade, we may note that back in 1950 an income of $10,000 was enough to put a household into the top 5% bracket. By 1960, a family income of $10,000 merely put a household into the top 15% bracket.

Dividing all high-income household heads (as defined by the top 5%) into six major occupational groups, Dr. Miller noted that salaried managers and professionals, making up only 28% of the total in 1950, now account for almost half. (See Chart 14, p. 147.)

All other groups, including self-employed farmers, businessmen, and professionals, plus the white- and blue-collar "aristocrats of labor" like salesmen and plumbers, suffered equivalent declines in representation in the ranks of the top 5 percent. Whereas in 1950 they accounted for 72% of all members of the income elite, their percentage shrank to 52% in 1960. (See Charts 15, 16 and 17, pp. 149-153.)

Some observers regard the growing importance of a high-income "salariat" as evidence of the increasingly pervasive domination of our economic life by the big corporation at the expense of small business. That may be so, but of more importance is the fact that

> The big change is the persistent intrusion of brain power into the top 5 percent. The small businessman and the farmer have given way to the engineer, scientist, college professor, plant manager, and others who deal primarily with ideas, not things.*

Salaried managers and officials increased their relative standing among the affluent households almost as much as the salaried professionals, of whom two-thirds are scientists and engineers. And of the high-salaried managers, a considerable fraction (about 40%) were *technical* managers—men with the kind of technical training or job function that qualifies them for inclusion in the ranks of the technical elite. (See Charts 8 and 9, pp. 135, 137.)

The role and growing importance of the technical manager in industry has received little attention from social scientists for lack of adequate data. This gap

---

* Herman P. Miller, *Rich Man, Poor Man* (New York: Crowell, 1964) p. 132.

has been filled in large part by a recent intensive survey* conducted by Henry L. Bass under the Science and Public Policy program of the Graduate School of Public Administration of Harvard University.

The sample was carefully drawn to represent all sectors of manufacturing activity, so that the percentages derived from the sample can be applied to a universe of some 260,000 salaried managers in manufacturing, reported by the 1960 census to have earned over $10,000. Each company participating in the survey (which included 69 of the nation's largest manufacturers) made random selections from among its own executives earning more than $10,000, who then answered the detailed questionnaires regarding their education and function.

The survey established for the first time the extraordinary degree of technical training characteristic of industrial management in the United States today. Of the total of 6380 managers polled, nearly half (45%) had at least one scientific or engineering degree. In addition, one in five managers had a graduate degree to supplement his technical bachelor's degree.

Managers with scientific or technical degrees were twice as numerous as those with nonscientific degrees (i.e., with majors in the social sciences, accounting and business administration, humanities, or law).

---

* Preliminary results from the study, entitled *The Education of Management in American Manufacturing,* have been published in *How Industry Buys #2* (New York: Scientific American, 1964).

Somewhat less than a third of all managers had no college degree at all, although most of these had some college schooling. The no-degree managers tended to be somewhat older, having a median age of 48 years in contrast to the median age of 44 for holders of degrees.

The possession of a technical education turns out to be inversely correlated with age to a remarkable degree. Of managers in the 35-to-39 age group, 53% had degrees in science or engineering. This percentage declined steadily as the age of the manager rose: in the 55-to-65 year age group, 36% had technical degrees (See Chart 10, p. 139).

Two-thirds of all managers with technical degrees were engaged in technical functions, i.e., those who worked in research and development, production, engineering, design, and quality control. Yet a considerable proportion—16% of all managers—had technical degrees but discharged nontechnical functions, involving either administration, sales, promotion, finance, or public relations. We include such managers in our measurement of a technical elite, for they play a strategic role in straddling the gap between the "two cultures" represented by the world of the scientist and engineer and that of the businessman.

Thus if we define technical management as composed of those managers with technical degrees regardless of function performed plus all those with technical functions regardless of education, we account for six out of every ten managers in manufacturing.

We can understand the profound importance of the technical manager when we examine that prime indicator of rank and authority—the industrial purchasing function. Two-thirds of all managers in the Harvard sample reported that they participated in the purchase of plant and equipment, materials, and components; of these, seven out of every ten were technical managers as defined above.

We can get some idea of what this means in terms of the industrial purchasing power deployed per man by applying these percentages to the "universe" of all manufacturing activity, from which the Harvard sample was drawn. The Bureau of the Census reported that in 1961 all manufacturing establishments spent about $216 billion for materials, components, plant and equipment. We can assume on the basis of the Harvard study that some 154,000 high-salaried technical managers "participated" in these expenditures, which gives each a shared responsibility for spending on the average more than $1 million a year!

Actually this is an oversimplification of the modern industrial purchasing function, which we know to be generally a team decision reflecting many different kinds of expertise. In the early stages, when basic questions of design and technical specifications are being determined, the scientists, engineers, and technical managers dominate. Other management echelons, including purchasing and financial management,

66

enter the picture in the later stages when price and other nontechnical factors remain to be settled.*

What is the relation of the scientist and engineer to the technical manager? About half of the managers with technical degrees in the Harvard sample reported that their first job was that of a scientist or engineer. We also know that the typical technical manager (median age 45) is much older than the typical scientist or engineer, whose median ages were reported in the 1960 census to be respectively 36 and 38. It seems clear, then, that half of the technical managers were former scientists or engineers who elected to go into management positions. It is frequently difficult for government agencies to decide whether to classify a person as a scientist or an engineer or a salaried manager.† At any rate, the easy interchange among these three categories underlines the necessity of treating all three as integral components of the new technical elite.

The relative youth of scientists and engineers is a consequence of the fact that they have doubled in number in the past 10 years. Requiring more than average schooling, their entry into the labor force tends to be somewhat delayed. Hence more than two-thirds fall into the 25-to-45 age groups, which is in sharp contrast to the labor force as a whole, where

---

* Cf. *How Industry Buys* (New York: Scientific American, 1955).

† For example, the 1960 census reported far fewer natural scientists than did the National Science Foundation for that year, presumably because many scientists and engineers chose to report themselves under occupational classifications other than that of "scientist."

less than half its members are in this particularly productive age bracket.

As would be expected, all members of the technical elite are highly educated. In contrast to the fact that only one out of every 10 members of the male labor force between the ages of 25 and 65 has a college degree, the corresponding ratio was better than three out of four for persons reporting themselves to the 1960 census as natural scientists. This ratio holds also for high-salaried technical managers in manufacturing. Curiously, only 56% of all persons reporting themselves to the Census Bureau as engineers had college degrees, reflecting perhaps the difficulty in accepting at face value such a self-designated professional status. However, about one in five of the 800,000 engineers over 24 years old covered in the census had graduate schooling, as did 44% of the natural scientists. Of the 200,000 scientists registered with the National Science Foundation in 1961, about one-third had doctoral degrees, and one-quarter of all high-paid technical managers in manufacturing had graduate schooling.

Census breakdowns of scientists and engineers by color and sex suggest the existence of large untapped future reserves of technical manpower. Women make up about one-third of the labor force today, but the 1960 census turned up only 22,000 female scientists and engineers, about 2% of the total. Yet, with respect to mathematics and biology, the two scientific fields now undergoing the most rapid expansion, women

68

accounted for more than one out of every four scientists reporting to the Census Bureau. Women today get somewhat more pre-college schooling than do boys, but far fewer bright girls go on to college. Since the average age at which a doctoral degree is awarded today is 30, the current trend toward early marriage cuts sharply into the number of women able to complete their technical training.*

Only 17,000 nonwhite scientists and engineers were reported in 1960, far below the 2% mark. The greatest numbers were in chemistry, where nonwhites made up 3.4% of the total. Since nonwhites in the United States account for 10% of total population, the indicated waste of untapped technical manpower is obvious.†

The combination of relative youth, affluence, and education confers on the technical elite a rather distinctive behavior pattern as sophisticated consumers of a broad range of quality goods and services. The magazine *Scientific American* describes its typical subscriber as follows:‡

Despite his high income, he is not a big saver;

---

* It may be noted that women in the Soviet Union make up 29% of all "engineer specialists with higher education," 76% of all medical doctors, and about one-half of the over-all technical work force. Cf. E. McCrensky, *Scientific Manpower in Europe* (New York: Pergamon Press, 1958) p. 156.

† A note of irony is offered in a news article from the *Wall Street Journal* (April 14, 1964) reporting a very great demand for Negro engineers "due to the 1961 Presidential order requiring firms doing business with the government to pledge not to discriminate in hiring."

‡ *Subscriber Portrait No. 59* (New York: Scientific American, 1963).

his portfolio of stocks and bonds is, if anything, below average for his income bracket. On the other hand, his purchases of ordinary and term life insurance are extraordinarily high, apparently based on the realization that his one real asset resides in his brain power, which must be insured. His professional involvements are such that he gives little thought to plans for retirement.

His expenditure pattern, therefore, reflects his interest in the current satisfaction of fairly expensive but discriminating tastes.

He is an inveterate traveler, both at home and abroad, for both business and pleasure. He has, probably, the highest ratio of coast-to-coast flights of any group in the country.*

In addition to travel abroad, his preference in cars runs very much to imports, sport cars, compacts, and to the upper price ranges. His technical background makes him conscious of quality workmanship in cars, high-fidelity audio equipment, cameras, and other expensive consumer goods. His high ownership of cameras also reflects his relatively early stage in the "life cycle" of consumers. He has young children, not yet out of their teens. He is particularly conscious of

---

* This appears to reflect the high concentration of the technical elite in California, New York, Massachusetts, and Washington, D. C., with 31% of all scientists and engineers as against 21% of total population.

their educational requirements. Books and music play an unusually important role in his life.

He prefers high-fidelity components to console models, and is the first to respond to new technical advances. Thus, about one-third of all subscribers own stereo equipment, nearly one-half own FM receivers, and a considerable proportion already own multiplex tuners.

We now have, in recent National Science Foundation surveys, considerable data on the distribution of the technical elite in industry. For example, as of January, 1961, the NSF reported on some 815,000 scientists, engineers, and technical managers* employed in manufacturing and nonmanufacturing establishments outside of the government and universities.

Here are some findings:

About six out of ten are in manufacturing, as against three out of ten in such nonmanufacturing categories as mining, construction, utilities, trade, and services.

More than half work in large establishments with over 1000 employees.

About two-thirds are engaged in research and development and in production, with the remaining

---

* Cf. *Scientific and Technical Personnel in Industry, 1961.* National Science Foundation, 63-32, Washington, 1964. Some technical managers were included here as scientists and engineers engaged in all technical and nontechnical functions. Technical managers without formal educational qualifications probably were not covered here.

one-third in management, sales, and other nontechnical activities.

The particular industrial concentrations within various technical areas of specialization are of some interest, too. Engineers, as the largest technical group, tend to be most evenly distributed over the entire range of industry, but with more than four out of ten concentrated in electronics, aerospace, and the machinery industries.

As might be expected, two out of five chemists are to be found in the chemical industries. About three out of ten physicists work in electrical equipment manufacturing, and one half of all metallurgists are concentrated in petroleum and natural gas extraction. Four out of five medical scientists, and three out of five biologists are concentrated in the drug and pharmaceutical industries. Plants producing foods and kindred products account for two out of five agricultural scientists. Three out of every five mathematicians are employed in the following industries: air craft and parts, finance, real estate and insurance (mainly actuaries), communications equipment, commercial laboratories and business and management consulting services, and office, computing and accounting machines.

The rapid spread of the computer to all phases of business is reflected in the distribution of mathematicians throughout all sectors of the economy. The wholesale and retail trades, which make the smallest direct claim on technology—they employ less than 4% of all scientists and engineers in industry—accounted for 7% of all mathematicians in 1961.

Although we have not included the social scientists among the technical elite, something should be said about the remarkable degree to which mathematics is increasingly affecting the work of economists, sociologists, psychologists, and marketing experts in industry today. Operations research, linear programming, econometric forecasting, sampling, simulation, game theory, and input-output analysis are a few of the terms used to describe ways in which mathematical techniques are being applied to the analysis of business problems today.

Input-output economics, for example, when allied to the computer, promises to put economic forecasting and industrial marketing on a truly scientific basis. Developed by Professor Wassily Leontief of Harvard University, input-output is a method of accounting for the numberless interchanges among all economic sectors and industries. Because high-speed computers can easily handle huge quantities of data, input-output tables will enable economic planners to evaluate the effects on hundreds of individual industries of any set of assumptions they care to make about the future. The analysis of industrial markets will be particularly facilitated by the ability of input-output studies to focus attention on the chain of relationships which reflects the state of the industrial arts at any given time.*

Finally, because of the computer the ranks of the technical elite have been swelled in the past 10 years by a new type of professional manager—the systems analyst, or data-processing expert. Census tabulations showed an annual gain of 16% between 1950 and 1960 in the number of persons in industry reporting themselves as "mathematicians," representing by far the highest recorded rate of gain in the demand for any single type of professional skill. It has been estimated that in 1964 some 50,000 persons were involved in the operation of nearly 20,000 computer installations in the United States as systems analysts and programmers, and a demand for 200,000 programmers is projected for 1970. Surveys of members of the Association for Computing Machinery indicate that the typical systems analyst is quite young (with a median age of 30), extremely well educated (most have already had some graduate training), and ambitious (most look forward to eventual top executive posts).†

The extreme youth of this new breed of technical workers is a reflection of the fact that computers have only recently begun to automate the traditional administrative functions of accounting, inventory

---

* Wassily Leontief, "The Structure of the American Economy," *Scientific American,* April, 1965, p. 25.

† *A Profile of the Programmer,* Deutsch & Shea Inc. (New York: Industrial Relations News, 1963).

control, marketing and sales analysis, as well as those involved in production and research. For this reason the computer expert is only beginning to ascend into the ranks of management. Yet it is clear that, as the computer succeeds in coordinating the automatic flow of all business information in the large corporation, the systems people designing this flow will be exercising an increasingly strategic function. They will therefore be logical candidates for future top corporate leadership posts, just as in the past comptrollers with accounting backgrounds found their way to the top by virtue of their knowledge of the over-all operation of all departments within the large modern corporation.

The administrative management function today is itself increasingly being oriented along quantitative, logical, and systematic lines, so that a "science of management" is truly coming into being. Newly developing information storage and retrieval systems, for example, can bring to the modern manager updated analyses of enormous amounts of raw data, machine-processed to facilitate his making highly sophisticated decisions.

For this purpose a new management discipline is emerging, called "information science." Combining the expertise of computer programmer, librarian, and documentation expert in coding, abstracting and indexing, the information scientist must grapple with the exponentially multiplying mountains of business and scientific information. New equipment and proc-

75

esses are being designed today to store information for ready access, including microfilm, thermoplastic and magnetic tape, and the related hardware, which will make the information scientist an indispensable member of management in the future.

On the other hand, the timid, conformist, yes-man genus of executive depicted in William H. Whyte's masterly study, *The Organization Man* (1956), is slated for replacement by the computer, which can make—far more quickly and cheaply—those routine, low level management kinds of decisions which do not require the spark of human creativity.

The technical domination of the middle echelons of corporate management which is implied in the foregoing discussion, was basically achieved in American industry in the decade of the fifties, as is traced in statistical detail in Charts 17, 18, 19, and 20, pp. 153-159. These charts can be summarized in the statement that at present two out of every three high-salaried professionals and managers (earning over $10,000 per year) in manufacturing can be included in the ranks of the technical elite, by virtue of either discharging technical functions in industry or having had technical training on the job or in college.

We come now to a key question raised first by Veblen: Has the technical elite, which now numbers one million persons in crucially responsible positions in industry, remained subordinate to the direction of men who know little and care less about technology, as Veblen charged? It is one of the great ironies of history that Veblen's distinction between the engineer and the modern captain of industry is being increasingly eroded today. As a result of the continuing scientific revolution of our time, new men are beginning to emerge at the very highest levels of command of America's leading corporations, men who speak the language not only of science and engineering but of business as well.

This shift in command, which Veblen despaired of seeing in his lifetime, can be read as confirming his view of the kind of leadership required by the basic logic and dynamic of modern technology.

VI THE NEW CAPTAINS
OF INDUSTRY

The continuing scientific explosion is not only creating a large technical elite, but from this pool more and more new men are rising into the top-most posts of industrial command.

The "new men" are not merely the result of a shift in names and faces. A composite portrait displays features of education, social origin, and intellectual outlook distinctly different from those of their predecessors. A survey made in 1963-1964 of the backgrounds and training of the two top officers of each of America's 600 leading companies—accounting for perhaps half of the national industrial output—revealed that nine out of ten came from poor or middle-income families, and that four out of ten have had college level or graduate training in a natural science or engineering or equivalent on-the-job training. This is an extraordinary social fact, in sharp contrast to previous eras in our national history and to the situation in England, France or West Germany.

Differing social and economic situations bring to the fore men of differing backgrounds and capacities. A classic study of the changing characteristics of American business leaders—their social origin, edu-

---

* The Big Business Executive; The Factors That Made Him, 1900-1950 (New York: Columbia University Press, 1955).

cation, inheritance of wealth, etc.—was published by Dr. Mabel Newcomer in 1955.* Dr. Newcomer examined biographical data for three generations of business leaders, in particular those who headed the largest American corporations in industry and trade in 1900, 1925, and 1950.

With the help of Dr. Newcomer, the writer shared the opportunity to question in a similar way about 1000 present-day corporate heads (Chairmen of the Board, Presidents, and Executive Vice Presidents) of the 600 largest American companies (those having over $100 million of sales in 1963).* Of these, 635 replied to, and commented on, some rather blunt and probing questions concerning their social and educational backgrounds and the role that family influence and other factors may have played in their business careers. Standard biographical reference works were used to garner as much data as possible for the remaining 357 officials.

The resulting data can be set in the context of a consistent trend of the increasing professionalization of big business leaders, traceable back to the turn of the century.

The most important finding is that only one out of ten corporate heads today comes from a rich family. The shift to poor or middle-income backgrounds has been particularly rapid in the past decade. In 1950,

---

* The results of this survey, discussed below, have been published in full in *The Big Business Executive*, 1964, (New York: Scientific American, 1965).

36% of all corporate heads queried by Dr. Newcomer had wealthy family backgrounds; but two generations before, around 1900, nearly half of all top business leaders came from wealthy families.

This indication of what sociologists call "upward social mobility" is supported, for example, by data on the occupations of fathers of present-day corporate heads. More than half of the fathers of the 1963 generation of business leaders were either employees or professional men—that is, they were salaried men or wage-earners or self-employed men from middle or lower-middle social levels. This certainly is evidence of a significant social change, for as recently as 1950, two-thirds of all corporate heads had dramatically different social origins: their fathers had been independent businessmen or had themselves been the heads of the same company later led by the sons. Thus the present is different indeed from what had been anticipated by social scientists in the 'thirties:

> . . . to the extent that business leaders of the present generation are drawn from the 'big business' class, inbreeding may be said to characterize the group responsible for the control and direction of American business. There is reason to believe that the representation of this class among business leaders is tending to increase as time goes on.*

---

* F. W. Taussig and S. C. Joslyn, *American Business Leaders* (New York: Macmillan, 1932).

One of the principal factors in this unanticipated development has been the increasing educational opportunities that have been available, particularly for men of poor and middle-income backgrounds. Ninety-one percent of company heads today have had some college education. This level is ten times greater than the corresponding percentage for their contemporaries. More than a third of the 1964 executives had graduate school training in contrast to 20% in 1950 and 10% in 1900; that is, only one in ten 50 years ago, but one in three today. It is equally clear that higher education is no longer a prerogative of wealth. In 1900, 71% of the corporate officials coming from poor backgrounds had only a grammar school education. The corresponding percentage in 1963 was 1.3%. And in 1964, one-third of all corporate heads from poor families had graduate school training, just as did those from wealthy families.

The third key finding is that the continuing professionalization of executives noted by Dr. Newcomer is becoming increasingly technical in character. Thus while the proportion of executives with college training more than doubled in the 63-year period, the sharpest gains were in science and engineering degrees. The percentage of corporate heads with technical degrees was below 7 in 1900, reached 20 by 1950, and shot up to 33 in the past decade. An additional 5% of the 1964 crop of corporate heads, including men like Edwin Land of the Polaroid Corporation and David Sarnoff of RCA, had no formal college degree in science or engineering but had sufficient on-the-job training to be regarded as having come up through the "technical" ranks.

Those findings, incidentally, have been independently confirmed in the recent Harvard study of 6000 executives in American manufacturing companies, in which it was found that 36% of those in the 55-to-65 age group had technical degrees. And for those between the ages of 35 and 45, who constitute the pool out of which the corporate leaders of the future will be drawn, more than half had technical degrees.*

Finally, the trend toward technical training is shown to be correlated with increasing social mobility. Thus, of the 1964 generation of executives from "poor" backgrounds, 40% had technical training, whereas only 20% of those from "wealthy" families had technical training.

What is new here is a growing *technical* emphasis. The trend toward increasing professionalization of big business leaders has been under way since the turn of the century. It was implied by Adolph A. Berle and Gardner C. Means in their seminal study of *The Modern Corporation and Private Property* (1933), which showed that ownership and control must necessarily be divorced in a big corporation so that it can operate with the massive capital resources of thousands of "owners." Control must therefore be exercised by professional managers, whose personal

---

* See Chapter V, *supra* and *U. S. Industry Under New Management,* (New York: Scientific American, 1963).

ownership of their companies' stock could not be more than nominal.

Thus, when Dr. Newcomer classified corporation heads of 1900 by their principal occupational experience, only one out of five could be characterized as a "salaried administrator." By 1950, and again in 1964, two out of five fell into this category. (Those classified as "entrepreneurs, bankers, and capitalists," making up half of the 1900 generation, constitute less than 2% of the current generation of top business leaders.) It should be noted that the "salaried administrator" has made no gain since 1950, whereas the proportion of those corporate officials classified as "engineer or scientist" rose, as we have seen, from one out of five in 1950 to one out of three in 1964.

Key managerial decisions today rest increasingly on technical and scientific premises that impinge upon and frequently override financial, marketing, and other business considerations. One of the respondents to the survey, the president of a company with $150 million of annual sales and a possessor of a Master of Business Administration degree, stated that

> [his] lack of technical knowledge is a distinct handicap. To help overcome this, we have had a full-time senior corporate executive to advise me on the long-range implications of technological change.

Similarly, nearly 6 out of 10 of the corporation officials who lacked technical training in 1964 indicated that formal training in engineering or natural science would have been "especially helpful" in their positions.

The technical emphasis should not, of course, be exaggerated. The scientist-executive is subject to the same pressures of maintaining satisfactory profit levels as are nontechnical corporate managers. The technical men in the survey felt a great need for more grounding in the humanities and in the professional business and management skills. One company president, with a B.S. degree in engineering, said:

> Technical training was adequate, but most fortunately, I had a sound secondary education emphasizing the "humanities"—Latin, Greek, history, English. I am not sure but that this secondary academic course was not more valuable in the long pull than my engineering degree.

Another commented:

> Had I had the time and opportunity when in college to take more courses in fundamental engineering and geology it would have been helpful. Also, a course in accounting and business management would have been desirable . . . It seems to me anyone in an administrative job, after he has had training in one of the scientific or engineering courses, will find the rest of his knowledge a matter of self-education, else one would be in school forever.

85

When asked to comment on the "pivotal" factors in attaining their present position, the 1964 generation of business leaders were quite modest, considering their enormous responsibilities. Many attributed their success to the good fortune of being in the right place at the right time. Most were well aware of the dangers of specialization and the need to combine both technical and nontechnical skills. But the great range of their interests, and the intense curiosity they displayed in the changing world about them, suggest that the selective processes from which they emerged were on the whole strikingly effective.

One of the surprising results of the survey of present-day corporate heads was that as many as 15% of the respondents checked "initiative in organizing the company" among the pivotal factors in attaining their present positions. It is evident, then, that entry into the ranks of big business is still possible, even in the era of the giant corporation. This suggests that capital funds are readily available but that high-level brain power remains in short supply.

It is interesting to note that the late C. Wright Mills, in a somewhat similar study of the background of business leaders in the eighteenth and nineteenth centuries,* found that the upper classes were generally dominant throughout our history. However, he found that in the national economic expansion fol-

---

* C. Wright Mills, *"The American Business Elite: A Collective Portrait,"* reprinted in *Power, Politics and People* (New York: Oxford University Press) p. 110.

lowing the Civil War, able men from lower social and economic levels first began to rise into the ranks of business leadership in significant numbers. A century later, a similar influx of "new men" is taking place, under the impetus of the scientific revolution of our time.

Perhaps the time has come to discard some of the stereotypes of how big business supposedly operates, and the cliches about the conformist behavior of the "organization man" in American business. The truth is that corporate officials exhibit more and more the same diversity of interests and political beliefs as the public at large, in keeping perhaps with their diverse social origins.

One wonders, for example, what Veblen would make of a "big businessman" like the late John I. Snyder, head of U. S. Industries, a large manufacturer of automation equipment, included among the leading firms in America today. Mr. Snyder had a degree in economics and studied at the London School of Economics under Professor R. H. Tawney, whose position among English economists was not unlike that of Veblen in America. Mr. Snyder's firm, in the full pursuit of private profit, is successfully engaged in selling equipment designed to disemploy workers at maximum rates. In 1964, Mr. Snyder estimated that automation in America was eliminating jobs at the rate of 40,000 per week, and he believed that the social impact of such technological unemployment would require massive government intervention on a scale that would probably jolt Veblen himself. Mr. Snyder advocated federal government programs for early retirement, a shorter work week, a guaranteed annual wage, and large-scale public works.

Mr. Snyder's views were probably not widely shared among his corporate peers, but they can be noted, perhaps as further evidence of the fact that the large corporations are becoming sufficiently flexible to find, to develop, and to use in top positions men of ability, regardless of background or beliefs, to guide their industrial destinies in an era of great technological change.

VII THE NEW TECHNOLOGY
AND COMPETITION

It is now clear that World War II, and the development of the atom bomb in particular, effected a radical alteration in the relation of science to industry, because it dramatized the tremendous power that organized scientific research could bring to industry. The scientist of today has achieved much greater status than the engineer had in Veblen's time. He is courted and acclaimed and can command favored positions in business, government, and university circles.

One consequence of this change is that big business no longer finds it desirable or even possible to retard the development of technical innovations that were formerly regarded with fear because of their presumed unduly upsetting effects on the market, as was charged in the TNEC hearings.* Any observer of the furious pace of the research and development boom, now involving annual expenditures of the order of $15 billion, is aware that if there is one thing that the typical large American corporation does *not* do today it is to try to stem the tide of technical progress.

---

* A frequently cited example of the extreme technical conservatism of big business in the 'twenties was the failure of General Electric to develop fluorescent lighting for fear of undercutting its own dominant position in incandescent lighting.

Such attempts have proved futile, because the scientists responsible for the great breakthroughs turned out to be too independent and mobile to permit a slow and leisurely development rate.

The post-war history of the electronics industry is replete with examples of new companies being launched to exploit the ideas of scientists and engineers that may have been born or developed in the laboratories of competitors. Soon after the announcement of the transistor in 1948, two of its discoverers left Bell Laboratories: Dr. John Bardeen turned to teaching, and Dr. William Shockley formed his own company. Note, too, that Bell Laboratories itself did not attempt to develop the transistor but chose instead to grant licenses to all comers. Again, the Thompson Ramo Wooldridge Company, one of the largest of the new "space" corporations, with a current sales volume of $.5 billion, stemmed from the departure of two scientists—Drs. Simon Ramo and Dean Wooldridge—from Hughes Aircraft in the early 'fifties.

Nowadays key research and development scientists and engineers get a kind of tender loving care from the big corporations that would astound Veblen. Disaffected scientists, singly or sometimes in teams, can easily depart and set up shop for themselves with outside financing if they have new ideas they wish to pursue in a different setting. It has been alleged that Wall Street banking houses maintain detail men whose job it is to scour the brain centers of Cambridge, Massachusetts, and the San Francisco Bay and Peninsular areas just to discover who may be unhappy.

Business concerns are sometimes so dependent on the possession (or loss) of technical information that a new kind of industrial intelligence or espionage industry has boomed today, designed to pick the brains of well-placed technicians, by fair means or foul. So fast is the pace of technical advance that the large corporation seems increasingly reluctant to tip its hand to competitors by applying for patents on new products or processes. Patent protection is seen to be illusory; in the time taken by litigation, precious lead time may be dissipated. Some are inclined to think that rushing innovations to the market, to get a jump on competition, is a better business strategy.

Big business can also fall prey to technical obsolescence. It is sobering to reflect on the fact that back in the 'thirties IBM and Underwood shared equally in the sales of office equipment. But Underwood did little research and development on the changing technology of office automation and eventually shrank to the status of a corporate shell, valued mainly for its name, which had been an honored one in the history of American business enterprise.

Another development is the increasing diversification of large corporations today. This reflects an attempt to stay abreast of the new waves of technological change and to keep from having all their eggs

91

in a single basket. A recent National Bureau study*
suggests that nearly half of the products of the leading American manufacturing corporations today may
be in industries other than the one in which they
achieved their original dominance. This tendency en-
hances competition among the giants, as when IBM
must confront General Electric and RCA in the field
of computers.

Modern scientific research in the molecular and
atomic structure of materials constitutes a great
threat to many large producers of the traditional raw
materials. Today new plastics, along with new devel-
opments in glass, rubber, ceramics, and nonferrous
metals, have challenged the dominant position of
steel as the basic construction material.

The ascendance of the scientist and engineer into
all levels of corporate command clearly reflects, then,
the degree to which modern science is changing (or
upsetting) the rules of the game in business and industry. The new technical manager still needs all the
managerial and marketing skills held in disdain by
Veblen, but he must exercise these talents in a far
more technically complex market.

The emergence of a technical elite in the direction
of American business does not mean that the Veblenian conflict between the needs of modern technology
and the business view of how to maximize profits has
disappeared. For while business has found that there

---

* Michael Cort, *Diversification and Integration in American Industry*
(New York: National Bureau of Economic Research, 1962).

is plenty of profit to be made from the exploitation of science, it remains true, first, that there are other ways to make profits and, second, that some technical achievements may require too much time and investment to be profitable in either the short or the long run for any single firm, no matter how large.*

This seems to be the only explanation for many inconsistencies and paradoxes still to be found in the relation of the scientist to big business. For example, large corporations account for the employment of the bulk of the technical labor force in the United States.† Some economists have therefore come to regard big business as greatly accelerating new technical development, because only a large company has the resources to engage in the risks of exploring new technical areas:

> Thus, in the modern industry shared by a few large firms, size and the rewards accruing to market power combine to insure that resources for research and development will be available.

---

* An example of a technological venture too big even for the AT&T, Bell Laboratories, and Western Electric complex is Comsat, organized as a consortium of many domestic and foreign private and governmental interests to use satellites for overseas communication. Comsat is a stock market favorite because it is seen to rest on billions of dollars invested by the United States government in developing a missile technology.

† In January 1961, 407 private industrial companies with over 5000 employees accounted for four-fifths of all scientists and engineers engaged in research and development. *Research and Development in Industry, 1960,* National Science Foundation, Washington, D. C., 1963, p. 47.

The power that enables the firm to have some influence on prices insures that the resulting gains will not be passed on to the public by imitators (who have stood none of the costs of development) before the outlay for development can be recouped. In this way market power protects the incentive to technical development. The net of all this is that there must be some element of monopoly in an industry if it is to be progressive.*

Yet many of the very largest companies, particularly in the auto and steel industries, lag far behind small companies in their relative dependence on the employment of scientists and engineers to develop new products and processes. No satisfactory correlation has yet been found between size of firm and research expenditures. Within the same industry, it has been established that

. . . firms of about the same size engage in research and development to very varying degrees [and that] although small firms are less likely to spend money on research and development than large, when they do in fact engage in these activities, firms in the low-size groups appear to spend, on the average, in proportion to their size, as much as firms in the large-size groups.†

---

* John Kenneth Galbraith, *American Capitalism* (Boston: The Houghton Mifflin Co., 1952) p. 93.
† J. Jewkes, D. Sawers, and R. Stillerman, *The Sources of Invention* (New York: St. Martins Press, 1961) p. 157.

There is, of course, wide variation in the degree of importance attached by industry to research and development, which we noted above as being highly correlated with productivity. Some of this variation certainly reflects the concentrated channeling of federal research and development funds in the past decade to the electronics and aerospace industries. Some variation can be attributed to the nature of the industry itself. Thus the apparel industry, with its emphasis on fashion design, appears least likely to yield to the rationalization processes of modern technology. Yet it is clear that all the consumer goods industries, which (See Chart 12, p. 143) have lagged in the application of science, will ultimately achieve a fairly complete automation of production and will continue to bring to the market a wide range of new products. Thus, there is no "natural" technological reason for the synthetic fibers to be developed in the chemical industry rather than in the textile and apparel industries. As the technical sophistication of business leaders continues to spread, such variation in the employment of science in industry will undoubtedly diminish.

But short-term profit considerations do impel big business to put far greater stress on development than on basic research. This charge, now amply documented, is an extension to our own time of the basic Veblenian critique. In their classic study of the origins of 61 important twentieth-century inventions,

Jewkes, Sawers and Stillerman* found only 12 (or 20%) that came out of the laboratories of large corporations: nylon, the transistor, freon refrigerants, tetraethyl lead, television, detergents, krilium, polyethylene, neoprene, fluorescent lighting, the diesel-electric locomotive, and plexiglass. Independent inventors contributed more than half of the 61 major inventions, including air-conditioning, automatic transmission, cellophane, the jet engine, etc. In a more recent study of 27 major inventions of the post-war period, D. Hamberg found only seven (26%) that came from large industrial laboratories, including cold sterilization, terrelac, and Vitamin B_{12}.†

In recent years corporate activities have been increasingly decentralized. In the course of decentralization, research laboratories have come to emphasize the improvement of the products of the operating division to which the laboratory is assigned. Some large companies retain central laboratories to work on "basic research" problems, but the bulk of the research and development expenditures of industry is undoubtedly allocated to the "improvement" type of invention.‡

Ultimately an even more basic conflict will flow out of the corporate attempt to organize the process of invention itself. The truly creative innovator is

---

* Op. cit., p. 85.

† D. Hamberg, "Invention in the Industrial Research Laboratory," Journal of Political Economy, April 1963.

‡ Ibid.

96

by nature far too independent a spirit to fit easily into the table of organization of the large industrial laboratory, with its emphasis on directed research. The scientist's view of his relation to corporate research is reflected in the following complaint:

> [research directors sometimes] fail to realize that the scientific standing of a scientist is determined primarily by the opinion of the colleagues in his specialty throughout the world. Actions that enhance [this] standing may bear little or no relation to actions that enhance his corporate standing. To achieve recognition from his professional colleagues, he must communicate his research in the open literature, but publication in technical journals may be of little interest to a company or may even be damaging to it. To achieve company recognition, his research must lead to a marketable product or technique, but such research may not help his scientific reputation one whit. It is an error to think that all a creative scientist requires for happiness is to create. His creation exists scientifically only if he can communicate it to his peers for evaluation. He not only wants to communicate his research, he wants it, and therefore wants himself, to be thought of highly . . .*

At any rate, very few scientists of wide renown are to be found as employees in corporate industrial re-

---

* Letter to the editors, *Fortune,* February 1965, p. 102.

search laboratories today; a survey taken in 1955 concluded that most industrial scientists "don't know one another, nor are they known by anybody else."* It appears that the services of the really great men of science are available to business today generally only as consultants.

We may therefore conclude that business today, although it frequently uses science inadequately, probably needs the scientist more than the scientist needs business, and this is why the balance between them is being shifted in favor of the scientist, as was foreseen by Veblen.

In further summary we can say that much of what Veblen saw in the relationship between business and the creators of new technology is valid today. His analysis helps us understand the nature of the conflict between them and the direction in which the resolution of that conflict must move.

Of course, his analysis is vulnerable to the argument of those who, although they concede that increasingly the important business and economic decisions will rest on a better understanding of the new technology, nevertheless vigorously deny that this constitutes the Good Society. Especially so, they would say, if our technological triumphs result in contaminating the atmosphere and water supply with radioactive debris, indissoluble synthetic detergents, poisonous insecticides, pesticides, automotive exhaust and all the

---

* W. H. Whyte, *The Organization Man* (New York: Harcourt, Brace, 1956) p. 208.

other waste products of an advanced technology. And they would look askance at the steady, inexorable displacement of unskilled labor by machines in an increasingly polarized society run by a technical elite.

The first answer to this charge is that the harmful effects of an inadequate technology can only be overcome by a better technology. We understand the purely technical problems involved, let us say, in the elimination of automotive smog, or in restoring the viability of urban transit. But our political, social and economic institutions do not react quickly enough to adjust to a technology expanding at exponential rates.

But in any case it would be unfair to chide Veblen for failure to anticipate all the issues that now confront us. If Veblen were alive today he would surely add his sardonic dissent to that voiced by John K. Galbraith in *The Affluent Society* and Michael Harrington in *The Other America* (1963). And he would probably regard the current concentration of scientists and engineers in military research as a classic example of the misuse of science.

But his was the unique view of technology as the driving force underlying Western civilization. To be sure, its development was closely intertwined with the business enterprise system that developed simultaneously in Western Europe and America. But he also saw in technology a superior force that could mold the business enterprise system to its own requirements and, in the process, add considerably to its profitability.

99

The new technologically oriented captain of industry envisioned by Veblen is, like his nineteenth century counterpart, a Faust-like figure who might cry out "Zwei Seelen wohnen, ach! in meiner Brust," for he must carry within himself the warring disciplines of business and science. That this can be done successfully is proved by the meteoric rise in the postwar era of companies like IBM, Xerox, and Polaroid (so prized by Wall Street as "growth stocks"), whose managements display all the advertising, marketing, and merchandising skills traditionally associated with big business. But in these companies such skills are subordinate in importance to those required in making the right technological decisions at the right time, frequently at great risks, a behavior pattern that Veblen would not have expected of big business.

The fiercely competitive computer industry has witnessed scores of crucial "business" decisions based on technical evaluations of a rapidly changing technology. Within a decade computers have shifted from the large cumbersome "tube types" to several generations of compact high-speed "solid state" systems, with each new cycle of computers requiring huge investments in new hardware, and in the even more expensive and time-consuming reprogramming required by the incompatible new systems. Today the entire industry is awaiting with baited breath, the results of one of the greatest such gambles in American business history, as the International Business Machine Company is staking its dominant position (with 70% of the billion dollar market in annual computer rentals) on the success of its new "360" system.

The "360" computer embodies an 8-bit number code and other technical innovations marking a sharp break with all previous systems, but which can make the "360" the first to handle all business and scientific computational needs with equal ease and speed. Success will rest in large measure on the ability of a huge staff of IBM mathematicians and programmers to prepare a complex New Programming Language and the necessary compiler programs to cover all those already written in such computer languages as "Fortran," "Cobal," and "Algol." Success for the "360" can render obsolete all previous computer systems throughout the world, including those built in the past by IBM itself. And yet, new configurations of future computer systems are already on drawing boards, and in time they will eventually supersede even the "360" system.

VIII   THE FUTURE

The exponential growth of science, with its explosive effects on productivity and profitability, ensures that even the most backward ranks of big business will want to increase the role of technology in their activities. In point of fact, the unprecedented profitability of American business in the post-war period does reflect in large part the extent to which science has penetrated all economic sectors. Corporate profits (before taxes) rose from a $40 billion level in 1950 to $60 billions in the mid-'sixties. It may even be true that the new investment outlets constantly turned up by the post-war research and development boom have had much to do with the dampening of the business cycle in recent years.

Veblen would be impressed with the doubling in real per capita income that has taken place in the United States since 1920. He would regard this increase as a measure of the degree to which the benefits of technology have been passed on to the ultimate consumer, without being absorbed or wasted in the business system. He acknowledged even in his time that

> The result of a business-like management of industry for private gain in America has on the whole been a fairly high level of prosperity.

He ascribed this to the continued growth and spread of population, which furnished businessmen with a continually expanding market for goods.

> Hence the American business men have been in the fortunate position of not having to curtail the output of industry harshly and persistently on all points. . . . To their credit be it said, they have on the whole not hindered the country's prosperity beyond what the traffic would bear.*

Today foreign markets hold the greatest potential for the high technology products of American industry, because that is where the American margin of technical superiority can reap the largest rewards. Although exports constitute a rather minor percentage of the total output of the American economy, we now export more than one-fifth of the total output of the more advanced types of machinery, transportation equipment, and chemicals. Of even more importance in adding to the enormous profitability of American business enterprise abroad is the growth of sales of United States-owned overseas subsidiaries, which in 1963 reached the all-time record of $28 billion, and which again reflect the most advanced sectors of American technology. The purchases of American computers, for example, are generally made on the basis of an objective evaluation of price and quality in a highly competitive market. Such sales do not require the traditional military expressions of

---

* *The Vested Interests and the Common Man*, p. 98.

104

imperial power, Veblen thought, though he was skeptical that this view would prevail.

The shift in direction taken by the American corporate enterprise—one that credits and takes advantage of the contributions of Veblen's technologist —does not, to be sure, signify the emergence of a new social system. For this reason Veblen has never been embraced by the extreme political left, despite his acidulous scorn for big business. Veblen did not share the Marxist faith in the ability of the working class to effect a radical reorganization of society. In his opinion, Karl Marx's assertion that Labor Power was the sole creative factor in economic life was based on a study of the workings of a mid-nineteenth century system, when it was still possible

> to speak of industry as an affair of detachable factors and independent segments of work going on in severalty,

e.g., without adequate recognition of the role of the technologist in maintaining "the industrial system at large as a going concern."* With respect to America, at least, Veblen's argument becomes increasingly difficult to rebut as automation systematically reduces the role of labor, both quantitatively and qualitatively.

But Veblen offers little solace to those at the opposite end of the political spectrum, who would have as much trouble accepting his view that the fruits of

---

* *Absentee Ownership*, p. 271n.

modern civilization are conferred by a high-level technology which need not necessarily be joined forever with the business enterprise system. Thus Veblen has not only downgraded the role of labor among the factors of production; he also questioned the ultimate function of capital as seen in its traditional role. Where most economic historians interpret the rise of Western civilization in terms of the slow and painful accumulation of capital resources, Veblen offers the alternative view of the steady emergence of a technical work force. Succeeding generations of technologists can easily recreate capital equipment far superior to that of the past or the present, so that clearly society's most important resource is its body of developing technical knowledge.

In this context, the relative speed with which the Soviet Union and now Communist China have been able to develop a technical labor force able to create a sophisticated nuclear technology gives Veblen's thesis a somber validation.

It is worth examining the way in which the Soviet Union has so quickly assembled a massive technical work-force, for here we see a conflict between science and another mode of social and economic organization. Seven years after Sputnik, Americans are no longer surprised to learn that as of 1960, the technical manpower resources of the Soviet Union nearly matched our own. Thus, as against 822,000 engineers in the U.S. in 1960, Russia had 973,000 "engineering and industrial specialists with professional training," plus 248,000 similar specialists in agriculture. Included here are the equivalent of several hundred thousand persons with technical training who exercise managerial functions, so that a rough equivalence with the U.S. is indicated. However, as against 335,000 natural scientists in the U.S. in 1960, Russia had about 250,000 physical scientists classified as RAP'S or employees in higher education and research institutions.*

This huge technical work-force did not however, come into being spontaneously; Russian science has a long and notable background. The Russian scientific tradition largely parallels that of the U.S. (as depicted in Chapter III), extending back to the establishment of the St. Petersburg Academy of Science in 1725 by Peter the Great, under the guidance of Leibniz, and originally staffed with such eminent foreign scientists as the mathematicians Bernoulli and Leonard Euler. Among the first Russian scientists of the 18th century were Leontii Magnitskii, who published a mathematics textbook as far back as 1703; Johann Gmelin, whose *Flora Sibirica* appeared at about the same time that John Bartram was discovering the flora of the New World; the mathematicians Kotelnikov and Rumovskii, both disciples of Euler; and of course the great Lomonosov, who could be regarded as the Russian counterpart of Benjamin Franklin. Like Franklin, Mikhail Lomonosov's inter-

---

* Nicholas DeWitt, *Education and Professional Training in the Soviet Union* (Washington: National Science Foundation, 1961) p. 409.

ests extended to all branches of knowledge; he was a "historian, theoretician, mechanician, chemist, mineralogist, artist and poet," and was the first man to envisage a science of physical chemistry.*

Paralleling the emergence of a technical work force in America, the Russian corps of scientists and engineers increased in numbers in the 18th and 19th centuries at an exponential rate that was somewhat more moderate than the 7 or 8% annual growth achieved in America in these years.

Thus in 1914 the number of RAP'S (senior academic and research personnel) was officially estimated at 10,200, although Nicholas DeWitt believes the true figure to be probably "two or three times greater."†

Allowing for such understatement, and for those RAP'S in the physical sciences, and for an equivalent complementing corps of engineers, it is clear that on the eve of the revolution, Russia had a not inconsiderable technical work-force of perhaps 25,000 persons which although about one quarter of the magnitude of the corresponding American technical work-force at that time, did represent the fruits of two centuries of a steady exponential annual growth rate of the order of 5%.

War and revolution interrupt the statistical record in the succeeding decade, and it is only since 1926

---

* Alexander Vucinich, *Science in Russian Culture* (Stanford: Stanford University Press, 1963).
† DeWitt, *op. cit.*, p. 415.

that we can trace the growth rates involved in the establishment of the present day technical work-force in Russia. But, it is clear that in the period since 1926, the Russians have achieved a remarkable doubling of the traditional 5% annual growth rates. Thus, from 1926-1959 the number of "engineers, technicians and agronomy specialists" (including persons with a semi-professional degree of training) multiplied 18 times, equivalent to an annual growth rate of 9%. And in these years, the number of research workers and academic personnel multiplied 23 times, equal to a 10% annual growth rate. In contrast to this technical emphasis, persons with college degrees in the humanities, arts and social sciences, excluding education, accounted for well under 10% of all Russian college graduates throughout these years.[*]

The achievement of a technical parity with the U.S. may permit the Russians to slacken its future rate of development of technical manpower, if only because they are evidently encountering great difficulties in making efficient use of their present large technical work-force in production. According to the Yugoslav scientist, Professor Stevan Dedijer, now at the University of Lund in Sweden, these difficulties stem from the official Marxist dogma that science was *not* part of the productive forces, but was rather "a part of the social superstructure consisting of the state,

---

[*] DeWitt, *op. cit.*, p. 483.

law, art, philosophy, ideology, all of which depend upon and follow the changes in productive forces."*

The Russian reluctance to admit that science was a productive force, for fear of thereby down-grading the role of the working class, was reflected in the suspicion with which they regarded the writings of Thorstein Veblen. Here is how the *Great Soviet Encyclopedia* describes him:

> Veblen proceeded from Kant's philosophic ideas, combining them with American pragmatism, and advocated an idealistic emphasis on the primacy of psychological factors in economic development. Hypocritically offering a demagogic "criticism" of capitalism and an acknowledgement of some of its defects, Veblen was in reality an enemy of Marxism, a zealous defender of capitalism, and looked for ways of saving it with the help of several "reforms," which did not affect the foundations of the capitalist system. These reforms provided for the creation of a "council of technicians" which would be nothing more than an instrument of the domination of the workers by the bourgeoisie. The reactionary program of technocracy was subsequently welcomed by other "reformers," but is merely a special form of bourgeois apologetics. . . .

But in recent years the Russians have evidently concluded that science is a directly productive force

---

* Stevan Dedijer, "Soviets Take a New Look At Science," *Bulletin of Atomic Scientists,* March 1965, p. 40.

and that the separation of science from production was artificial, and was responsible for the embarrassing fact that the productivity of the Russian technical work force was only half that of the U.S. Most estimates of the current relation of Soviet output to that of the U.S. run between 40 and 60 percent. At either figure it is clear that judged by American standards, the work of the huge Russian technical corps is being inadequately reflected in current production levels. The case could not have been more plainly stated than in the following excerpt from a speech of Khrushchev in 1956:

> The separation of research activity of the Academy of Sciences, departmental research institutes and higher educational establishments can no longer be tolerated. This separation and lack of coordination prevent the concentration of research activity on the solution of major scientific and engineering problems, lead to duplication of effort and waste of resources, and retard the introduction of research and engineering achievements into production.*

Since 1956 the Russians have instituted a series of re-organizations designed to decentralize research and get the scientist into the plant. While some success has been achieved in this regard, Prof. Dedijer, a friendly but objective observer could still state:

"The current state of interaction of science and

---

* Quoted in DeWitt, *op. cit.*, p. 430.

society in the Soviet Union can be said to suffer from the following weaknesses: an unbalanced development of some key research fields; no substitute having been found for the profit motive, Soviet industrial and agricultural enterprises are not innovation oriented and hence not research oriented; the scientific community does not act as an autonomous force in the formulation and execution of science policy; being too tied to ideology and current politics, Soviet social science suffers from lack of freedom to choose problems and methods of research.*

In recent years, the Russians have come to see that the problem may not be so much with the scientist himself, who can be fairly easily directed into alternative uses of his technical skills, but rather with the plant manager who must be induced, perhaps with the lure of a profit motive, to integrate the scientist into the production process at the plant level. Accordingly, following the theories of the Russian economist Yevsei Liberman, some tentative steps have been taken to remove some plants from the restrictions of a centrally planned output goal, so that they may enjoy the latitude of responding to the relatively free play of forces of supply and demand. In this way it is hoped, Russian plant managers will, like Veblen's cap-

---

* *Op. cit.,* p. 41.

tains of industry, be alert to opportunities to introduce technological innovations in a natural and truly creative manner; in short, along the lines of American experience.

A bitter debate is now proceeding in the Soviet Union on the advantages and dangers of opening the Pandora's box of a profit motive in industry. The dangers would presumably come from the possible limitations that a free market could set on output levels. In such an argument it is likely that the Russian scientist would remain neutral, letting the economists decide whether the inefficiencies in the utilization of his services are greater under a central plan than those involved in having the plant produce for profit.

It is interesting however to note the Veblenian overtones in the way in which Professor Liberman both extolls and attacks the role of profit in the determination of the efficiency of enterprise. In a recent article revealingly entitled "Are We Flirting With Capitalism?",* Professor Liberman praises profit as

> "a necessary yardstick of production efficiency [which] generalizes all aspects of operation, including quality of output. The prices of better articles have to be correspondingly higher than those of articles that are outmoded and not properly suited to their purpose . . ."

---

* "Soviet Life," June 1965, p. 36-39.

On the other hand, Professor Liberman also sees great dangers in such a use of the profit margin when, as under private enterprise,

> "high profits come most readily from advantageous buying of raw materials, the raising of retail prices, the tendency of unemployment to lower wages, nonequivalent exchange with developing countries, the system of preferential tariffs and custom duties, raising the prices of stocks on the stock exchange, and so-called Grunder (speculators) profits."

Since such factors presumably do not operate in the Soviet Union, Professor Liberman implies that only under a controlled plan could profit truly function as an indicator of production efficiency. Yet he readily concedes that in his country "profit was not and still is not used as the major indicator of the efficient operation of our enterprise."

And indeed, Professor Liberman does not explain how profit could be used in this way, if for example an enterprise cannot disemploy workers displaced by improvements in plant efficiency or by technical innovation. Or again, how is one to distinguish the "advantageous buying of raw materials" (presumably bad) from the praiseworthy recognition and exploitation of new materials which displace those "outmoded and not properly suited to their purpose"?

It is clear that Russian economists are only beginning to grapple with the true nature of the paradoxical tie that binds the truly efficient management of enterprise, capable of assuming risks when necessary, to the unmanageable and disruptive force of scientific creativity, which cannot really be planned.

Veblen too saw the interests of management and of science as divergent, but saw in the profit margin a device to harness the energies of both to the task of advancing economic development. It may be that the Russians too will come to accept the use of profit for this purpose, perhaps within some more or less flexible framework provided by a central plan.

Professor Dedijer's forecasts for Russia are of interest here:

"In my opinion, the new Soviet ideology of science policy, based on the idea that research is "a direct productive force" will tend to change the present state of interaction of science and Soviet society in the following directions: the social and political status of research work, of researchers, and of the scientific community will increase; social priority for research in general and for basic research in particular will increase; the socialization of science will increase; which may help bring about the invention of a substitute for a profit motive; there will be more intense study by the social sciences of the problems of the growth of science and its interaction with society; and finally, a definite program of action based on the new ideas about science will emerge."

115

The managers of Soviet industrial trusts may some day be permitted to exercise initiative in the use of modern scientific managerial techniques to maximize the profits of their enterprise. And if the framework of the central plan controlling their activity is not too constrictive, they will perforce make increasing use, for example, of management techniques which increase the efficiency of *distribution* of the products of industry: traffic management, the optimum location of plant and warehouse facilities, plus the use of brokers and other wholesaling intermediaries to facilitate inter-industry communication and the reporting of existing reserves and deficits, and even the principles of merchandising, packaging, market research and advertising.

Western experience has amply demonstrated that very high levels of efficient operation can be achieved by managers with profit incentives but little or no ownership interest in their companies.* In time then there will perhaps be an increasingly close resemblance with the West, at least outwardly, with respect to the way in which the management of socialist enterprise develops and exercises both a technical and a business expertise.

Veblen would probably regard the Russian emphasis on science as highly realistic, and their difficulties

---

* For example the largest corporate enterprise in Italy, ranking close in sales volume to such European giants as Royal Dutch/Shell and Unilever is the state-owned Istituto per la Ricostruzione Industriale (IRI), which runs much of Italy's public utilities, and accounts for major shares of Italy's output of steel, gas, cars, ships, etc. . . .

in the use of planning techniques as against profit incentives as reflecting the adaptations that all social systems must experiment with to satisfy the needs of an advancing science. He would probably see both systems, that of free enterprise and socialism, as alternative socio-economic attempts to live with, and exploit the great productive power inherent in science, which he saw as an autonomous force above ideology. The fact that at different stages one system would emphasize research over development or centralization over decentralization while the other would reverse the order of priority, would matter little. The specific way in which each system would find it necessary to adapt itself to this powerful force pales into insignificance when measured against the force itself.

The case can be put in even stronger terms by peering into the future: by the year 2000, both the Soviet Union and the U.S. will be able to deploy armies of scientists and engineers numbering in each case between 3 and 4 million persons. The output levels that could be generated in each case would stagger the imagination, and could certainly go far to meet the equally staggering needs of that part of the world which remained underdeveloped. It is easy to speculate that in each case, the social superstructures would be powerfully affected, albeit in specific ways difficult to foresee, by the capacity of each system to make any kind of relatively efficient use of the powerful productive forces at its disposal. One long range prediction that both Henry Adams and Thorstein

117

Veblen would make is that long after the specific modes of social and economic organization employed by mankind in the 20th century have become artifacts of interest only to archeologists, the productive powers of mankind will still be multiplying with the continuing advance of scientific knowledge. For man's capacity to extend his understanding of nature is a universal aspect of the human condition, and will outlast all specific forms of social organization.

Coming back to the present, Veblen's future supporters will perhaps come mainly from the ranks of those who accept the truth that modern technology has after all, reached its highest levels in association with the business enterprise system, and in this context will continue to score new technical triumphs. But we now live in a world in which the "secrets" of modern technology are increasingly open to all peoples, and to those living under other social and economic systems. The future successes of the enterprise system will therefore increasingly depend on how the Veblenian conflict between business and science is resolved, while we leave the Russians to reconcile science with central planning. In each case, the ultimate test of a Good Society will include among others, the criterion that human intelligence be used most effectively and efficiently in providing the nation's goods and services.

CHARTS

Chart 1

GROWTH IN THE NUMBER OF SCIENTISTS AND ENGINEERS, 1750-2000

These estimates of the number of natural scientists and engineers in the years 1900-1960 are based primarily on Census and National Science Foundation data, but are supported too by membership records of scientific and engineering societies. They show a vigorous exponential growth, which conforms closely to a theoretical exponential pattern extending over nearly three centuries. While a slight retardation seems evident in the later decades, the persistent exponential growth should result in at least 3.5 million scientists and engineers in the U.S. by the close of the 20th century. (See Appendix)

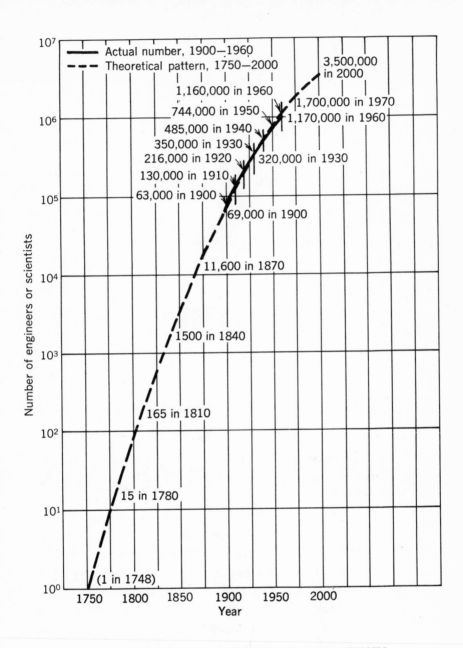

GROWTH IN THE NUMBER OF SCIENTISTS
AND ENGINEERS, 1750-2000

121

CHART 2

GROWTH IN THE NUMBER OF SCIENTISTS AND ENGINEERS BY TYPE, 1900-1960

Exponential growth patterns now characterize almost all branches of the natural sciences and engineering. The "newer" disciplines—physics, including mathematics, and biology, show somewhat more rapid growth than the "older" fields in engineering and chemistry.

The estimates plotted here have been derived by reference to membership records of various technical societies. (See Appendix)

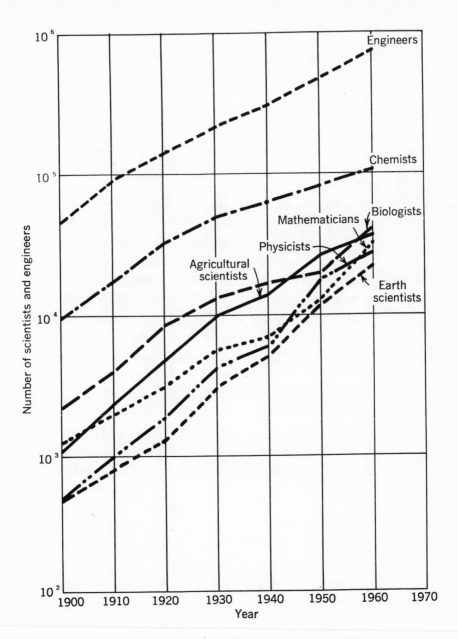

GROWTH IN THE NUMBER OF SCIENTISTS
AND ENGINEERS BY TYPE, 1900-1960

CHART 3

GROWTH IN THE NUMBER OF SCIENTISTS AND ENGINEERS

The accelerating historical impact of the exponential growth of the scientific and technical work force can be dramatized by adopting a device first used by Henry Adams, in which a logarithmic scale is applied along the horizontal time axis, rather than along the vertical axis as in Chart 1. This accords with our psychological perception that in the measurement of science and other related areas of the development of human thought, what has happened in the most recent period is far more important than the same interval further back in time. For example, as Adams noted, beginning at least 50,000 years ago, there has been a steady shrinkage of time intervals between the discovery of one form of energy after another—of fire, water, wind, steam and the combustion engine. Wind power has been used for the past 1000 years, steam power for more than two centuries, the combustion engine for less than a century, while in the past decade nuclear reactors have started to deliver electricity to power networks. Taking 1960 as "the present" and plotting the number of scientists and engineers on such a chart yields a J shaped curve which forcefully conveys a sense of the "acceleration of history" and the wide gulf separating the onrushing future from the past.

124

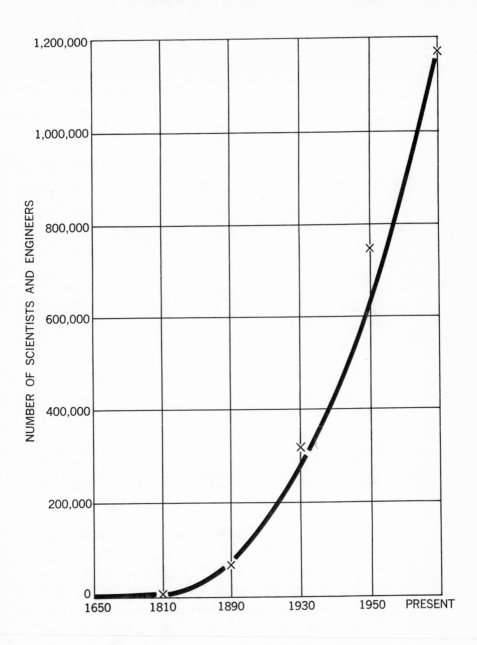

GROWTH IN THE NUMBER OF SCIENTISTS
AND ENGINEERS

Chart 4

U. S. MANUFACTURING OUTPUT, 1950-1960

Manufacturing output in the U. S. rose by 43% in the 1950-1960 decade, according to the Federal Reserve Board Index of Manufacturing Output. Over the period 1950-1964 the indicated gain is of the order of 70%, but we shall center attention on the 1950-1960 decade in order to make use in subsequent charts of considerable detail on the changing composition of the manufacturing labor force available from 1950 and 1960 Census Bureau tabulations.

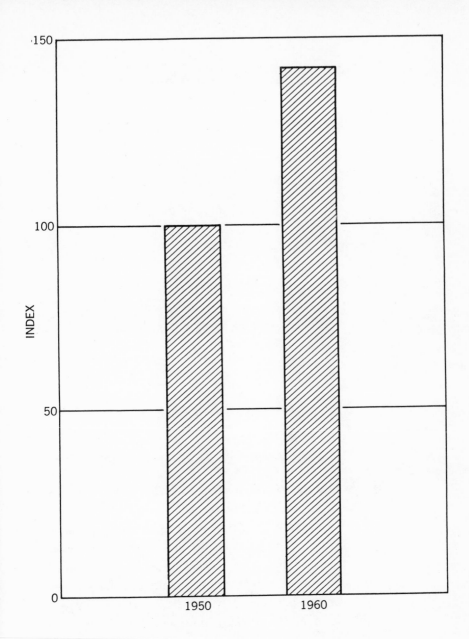

U. S. MANUFACTURING OUTPUT, 1950-1960

Chart 5

U.S. BLUE COLLAR WORKERS IN MANUFACTURING, 1950-1960

According to the Bureau of Labor Statistics, the number of blue collar workers (i.e., production workers) paid mainly on a time basis remained unchanged in this period, so that output per production worker rose by more than 40%. Census estimates of the number of blue collar workers in manufacturing showed a slight gain between 1950 and 1960, but with a probable drop in the average number of weeks worked during the year sufficient to cancel out the increase in employment.

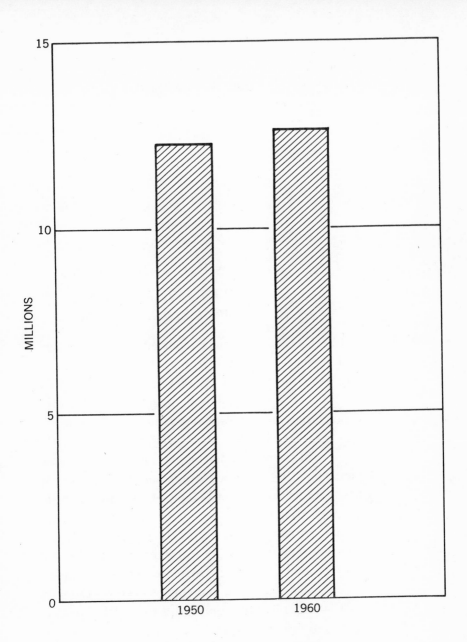

U. S. BLUE COLLAR WORKERS IN
MANUFACTURING, 1950-1960

129

Chart 6

U. S. ENGINEERS AND SCIENTISTS IN MANUFACTURING, 1950-1960

1960 Census tabulations reported 541,000 scientists and engineers employed in manufacturing, a gain of 80% over the figure of 292,000 reported by the 1950 census. This near doubling is roughly in line with the exponential growth rate observed for all engineers and scientists in the entire economy. Actually, the number of scientists and engineers reported in manufacturing in 1960 by the National Science Foundation post-censal survey was 614,000; 14% greater than the 1960 census figure.

As scientists and engineers extend their influence in industry they increasingly transfer to managerial and non-research functions. Therefore most of the additional 73,000 scientists and engineers enumerated by NSF were probably reported by the 1960 Census in managerial occupations.

Source: NSF Bulletin 63-64 *Scientists, Engineers, and Technicians in the 1960's*. Washington, D.C. 1964.

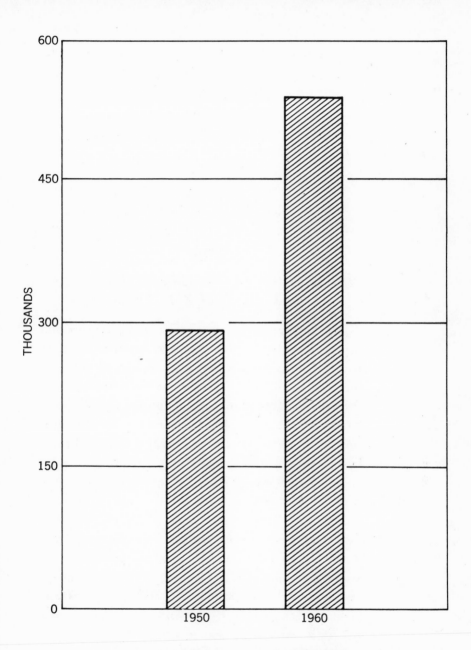

U. S. ENGINEERS AND SCIENTISTS
IN MANUFACTURING, 1950-1960

131

CHART 7

BREAKDOWN OF THE MANUFACTURING LABOR FORCE, 1950-1960

The doubling in the employment of scientists and engineers in manufacturing in this decade was almost matched by corresponding gains in the relative importance in industry of other white collar groups, particularly salaried managers, numbering 649,000 in 1960, a 70% gain over 1950. Other white collar groups (including other professionals, other nonsalaried managers, officials and proprietors, clerical and sales workers) rose from 2.7 million to 3.8 million, a gain of about 40%. All such gains decreased the relative importance of blue collar workers (craftsmen, foremen, operatives, service workers and laborers) from about 77% of the manufacturing labor force in 1950 to 71.6% in 1960. [If the Census data on blue collar employees, which totalled 12.6 million in 1960, as against 11.0 million in 1950, could be reduced to their full time equivalent, the decline in the blue collar component of the manufacturing labor force would be greater, to about 69% in 1960.]

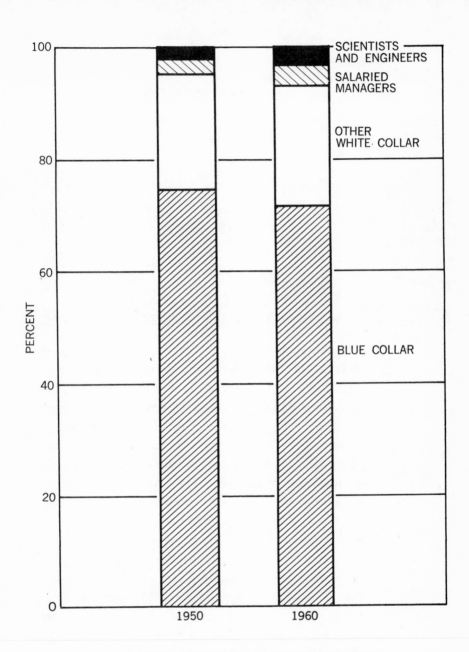

BREAKDOWN OF THE MANUFACTURING
LABOR FORCE, 1950-1960

CHART 8

CHARACTERISTICS OF SALARIED MANAGERS IN MANUFACTURING, 1961

Additional light can be focused on the growing importance of the salaried manager in manufacturing by means of a recent study of the educational background and functions of a sample of some 6300 managers (earning over $10,000) conducted by the Graduate School of Public Administration at Harvard, as part of its Science and Public Policy research program. Of all managers in the sample (drawn as representative of all manufacturing industries) 45% had college degrees in a natural science or engineering, while 15% without such degrees nevertheless discharged technical functions. (Technical functions include operation and production, engineering, design and development, research and quality control). Thus, by virtue either of education or function, about six out of ten salaried managers in manufacturing in 1961 (the date of the Harvard Study) can be considered members of technical management, i.e., of the "technical elite."

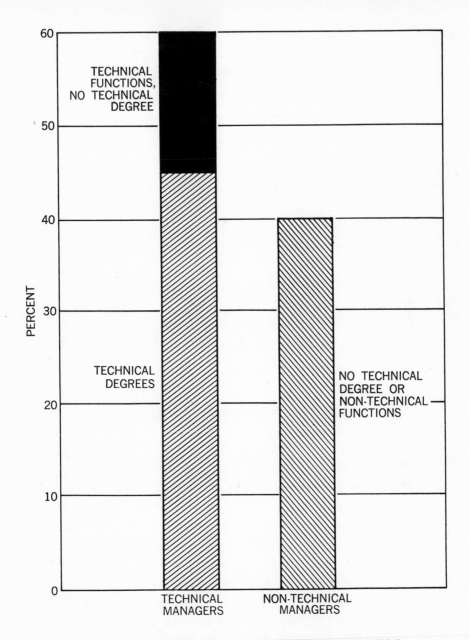

CHARACTERISTICS OF SALARIED MANAGERS
IN MANUFACTURING, 1961

135

CHART 9

PURCHASING RESPONSIBILITY OF TECHNICAL MANAGERS

Of the managers queried in the Harvard sample, two-thirds indicated personal participation in company purchasing. Among technical managers (as we have defined them), 79% indicated participation in purchasing, whereas only about half of the nontechnical managers indicated having such responsibility. Thus, judged by the strategic criterion of industrial purchasing power, the technical elite today represents a powerful influence in industry. The expenditures of U. S. manufacturing industries in which technical managers played a prime role totalled $228 billion in 1963, of which $11 billion represented capital expenditures (i.e., for plant and plant equipment) and the balance was about equally divided between components and materials.

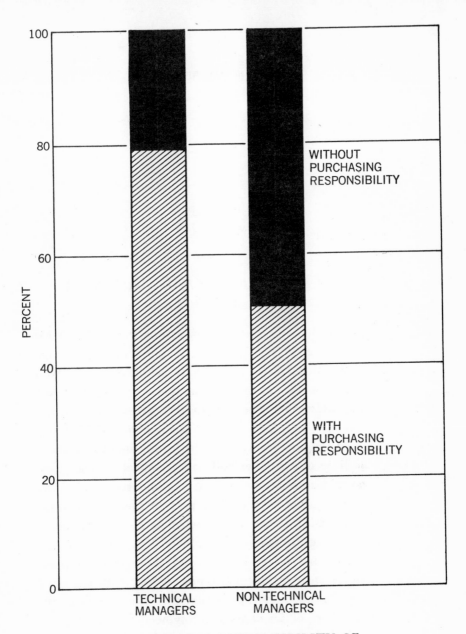

WITHOUT
PURCHASING
RESPONSIBILITY

WITH
PURCHASING
RESPONSIBILITY

PERCENT

TECHNICAL
MANAGERS

NON-TECHNICAL
MANAGERS

PURCHASING RESPONSIBILITY OF
TECHNICAL MANAGERS

137

CHART 10

AGE DISTRIBUTION OF TECHNICAL MANAGERS

Another interesting characteristic of the 6,000 managers in the Harvard sample concerns the age distribution of those who had technical degrees, who made up 45% of the total sample. For managers over 55, only 36% had technical degrees, but for the younger men between 35 and 45, who can be considered the pool from which the future top management will be drawn, over half had technical degrees. This strong correlation between age and technical training suggests that with respect to the 71% increase depicted in the total number of salaried managers in manufacturing between 1950 and 1960, an even larger gain must have characterized those younger managers with technical training. Other evidence, cited below, indicates that similarly to the growth in the numbers of scientists and engineers, the number of salaried managers in industry with technical training or function also doubled.

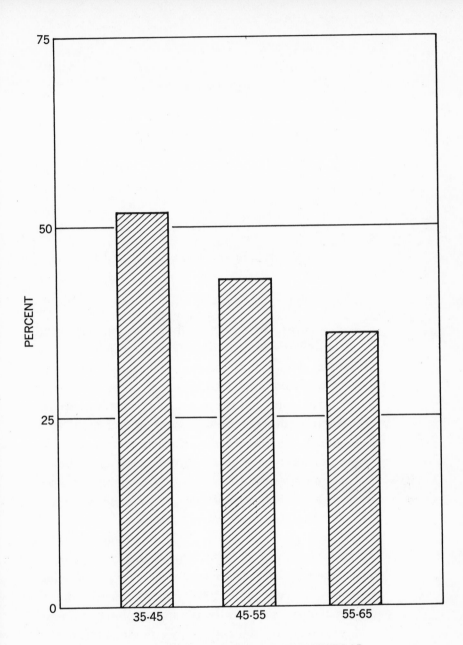

AGE DISTRIBUTION OF TECHNICAL
MANAGERS

139

CHART 11

TECHNICAL EMPLOYMENT AND PRODUCTIVITY: HIGH TECHNOLOGY INDUSTRIES

Here we show the close association between the employment of the technical elite in manufacturing and productivity gains. Productivity gain is measured here as the index of change in value-added per man in the period 1947-1961, calculated for each of 18 manufacturing industries defined according to the standard industrial classifications on a "2-digit" level of detail. On the scale on the left we measure, for each industry, the percentage of total employment (as reported in the 1960 Census) made up by scientists, engineers, technicians and salaried managers.

For all manufacturing industries in 1960, this percentage came to 8%. The "high technology" industries shown here all had technical employment ratios in excess of 10% and corresponding gains in productivity in excess of the 100% increase reported by all manufacturing. Even for the high-technology industries, there is a downward drift in the productivity measures apparent when the industries are ranged in the order of degree of technical employment.

140

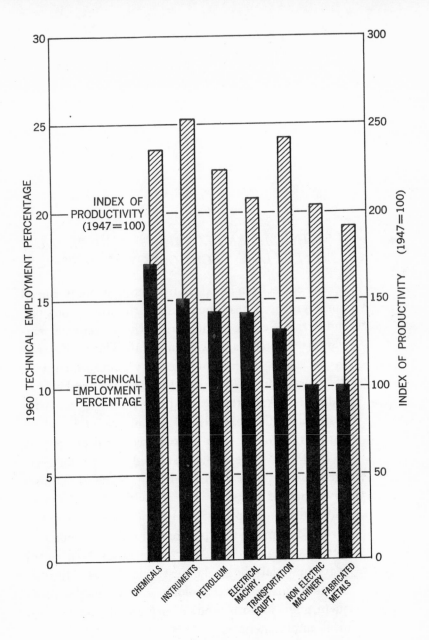

TECHNICAL EMPLOYMENT AND PRODUC-
TIVITY: HIGH TECHNOLOGY INDUSTRIES

141

CHART 12

TECHNICAL EMPLOYMENT AND PRODUC-
TIVITY: LOW TECHNOLOGY INDUSTRIES

The correlation between productivity and technical employment is also apparent for the low technology industries, i.e. those industries whose technical employment percentages were under 10. These industries in the aggregate had productivity gains which were 25% less than those enjoyed by the high technology industries, And, the correlation is seen to be fairly systematic. One exception is primary metals, which with a far smaller than average technical percentage in 1960 (5.8%) nevertheless scored better than average gains in value-added per man. Some economists have charged the steel industry with maintaining an "administrated" price structure in the 'fifties which diverged from the trends noted for industries not subject to so high a degree of concentration.* In recent years, however, the steel industry has invested heavily in modernizing its technology with probable subsequent gains in both productivity and degree of technical employment.

---

* Gardner C. Means, *The Corporate Revolution in America*, New York, Crowell Collier, 1962, Chapter 5.

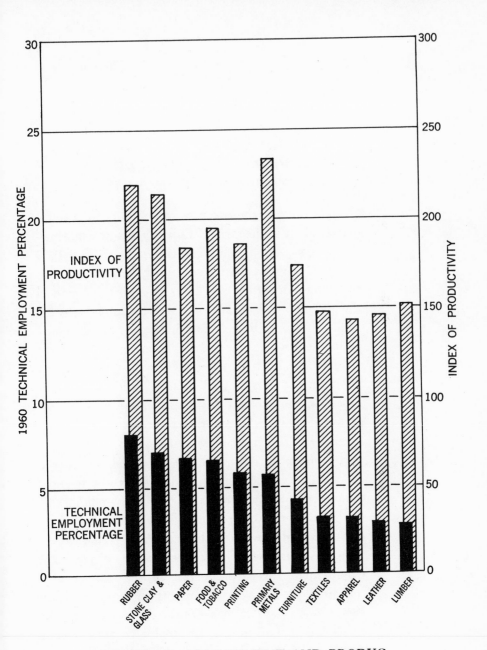

TECHNICAL EMPLOYMENT AND PRODUC-
TIVITY: LOW TECHNOLOGY INDUSTRIES

CHART 13

SUMMARY OF RELATION BETWEEN TECHNICAL EMPLOYMENT AND PRODUCTIVITY INCREASE

The results of the two previous charts can be summarized here in the form of a scatter-diagram in which for each two-digit manufacturing industry the 1960 technical employment percentage, and the corresponding percentage gain in value-added per man in the period 1947-1961 are plotted on a double-log scale. While there can be no question that in the post-war period as a whole, the greatest gains in productivity were scored by high technology industries, a much different picture is shown by a similar scatter-diagram based on the productivity gains in the most recent period 1958-1963, as reported in preliminary releases from the 1963 Census of Manufactures.

In this most recent period, if we eliminate the extraordinary productivity gain registered by the now almost completely automated petroleum refining industry, no consistent productivity advantage appears to be associated with the high technology industries, as against those with low concentrations of technical employment, in sharp contrast to the experience of the entire post war period. In both cases we are using 1960 Census data to measure the degree of technical employment, and are as yet unable to trace recent changes in such employment in the so-called low tech-

Continued on page 146

144

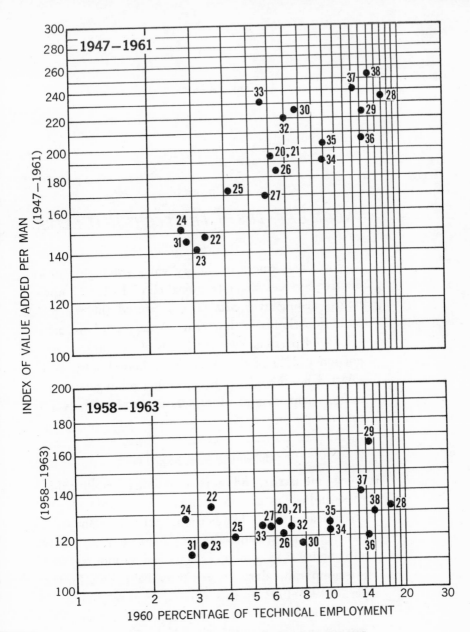

SUMMARY OF RELATION BETWEEN
TECHNICAL EMPLOYMENT AND
PRODUCTIVITY INCREASE

CHART 14

INCOME STATUS OF THE TECHNICAL ELITE
1950

How does American society value the highly productive services of the technical elite? In 1950 households earning over $10,000 constituted the top 5% of all households in that year. As depicted here, self-employed persons were the heads of the largest proportion (42%) of these privileged households, while salaried household heads, including managers, engineers, scientists and other salaried professionals accounted for only 28%.

Continued from page 144

nology industries, and there is a strong possibility that these industries are now undergoing a rapid rate of "technicalization." The National Science Foundation has begun to measure the employment of scientists and engineers in companies classified by industry but the comparable data are as yet available only for the period 1961-1962. In this interval small relative gains in technical employment were reported in foods and textiles and somewhat sharper declines in the defense-oriented electrical and transportation equipment in-

Continued on page 148

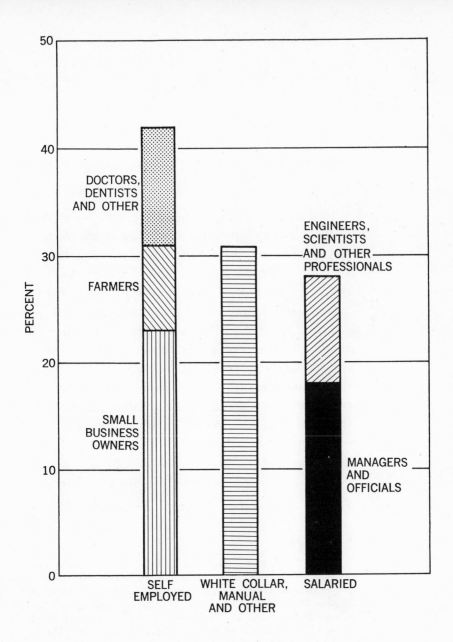

50

40

DOCTORS,
DENTISTS
AND OTHER

ENGINEERS,
SCIENTISTS
AND OTHER
PROFESSIONALS

30

FARMERS

PERCENT

20

SMALL
BUSINESS
OWNERS

MANAGERS
AND
OFFICIALS

10

0

SELF
EMPLOYED

WHITE COLLAR,
MANUAL
AND OTHER

SALARIED

INCOME STATUS OF THE TECHNICAL ELITE
1950

147

CHART 15

INCOME STATUS OF THE TECHNICAL ELITE
1960

In a single decade a complete reversal took place in the relative proportions of salaried versus the self-employed among the top 5% of income receivers. By 1960 a household income of $15,000 was necessary to qualify for the top 5%. Among these privileged households, salaried professionals and managers now accounted for 48%, while the percentage of self-employed household heads shrank to 26%. Here is the real "income revolution" of our time. As we shall show, two-thirds of the high income salaried professionals and managers are the scientists, engineers and technical managers, whose efforts in industry have proven to be so productive.

Continued from page 146

dustries. (Cf. National Science Foundation, "Scientific and Technical Personnel in Industry, 1962," NSF 64-34, p. 27).

NOTE. In these charts the various industries are denoted by their so-called two digit SIC number codes, used by the Census for purposes of classification, as follows: 20, Food; 21, Tobacco; 22, Textiles; 23, Apparel; 24, Lumber; 25, Furniture; 26, Paper; 27, Printing and Publishing; 28, Chemicals; 29, Petroleum; 30, Rubber; 31, Leather; 32, Stone, Clay and Glass; 33, Primary Metals; 34, Fabricated Metals; 35, Nonelectrical Machinery; 36, Electrical Machinery; 37, Transportation Equipment; 38, Instruments. A final heterogeneous Miscellaneous Industry grouping (39) is not shown here.

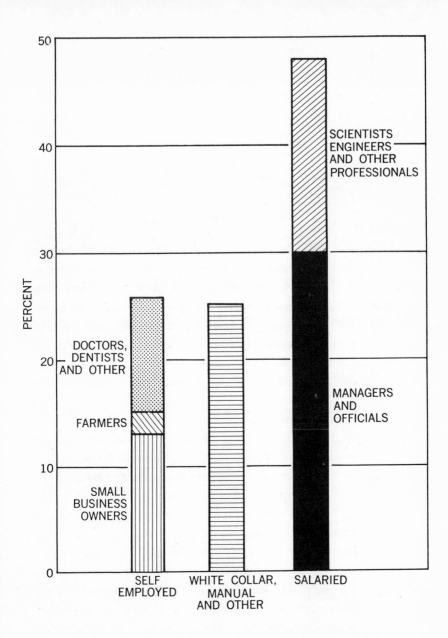

INCOME STATUS OF THE TECHNICAL ELITE
1960

CHART 16

INCOME STATUS OF THE TECHNICAL ELITE, 1950-1960 CHANGE

The transformation in the distribution of the top bracket of income earners is presented here in terms of the percentage change in the 1950's within each of the six major occupational groups of the labor force. Salaried managers, and the salaried technical and other professionals turn out to be the only occupational categories to score dramatic gains, for they nearly doubled their representation among the top 5%.

The representation among the top 5% of the self-employed farmer and businessman suffered declines in 1950-1960 almost as dramatic as the gains scored by the technical elite, who make up the bulk of the salaried managers and professionals employed at the high salaries necessary to fall into the top income brackets. Dr. Herman Miller of the Census Bureau, comments on this table as follows: "The big change is the persistent intrusion of brainpower into the top 5 percent. The small businessman and the farmer have given way to the engineer, scientist, college professor, plant manager, and others who deal primarily with ideas, not things." (*Rich Man, Poor Man*, Crowell, 1964 p. 132)

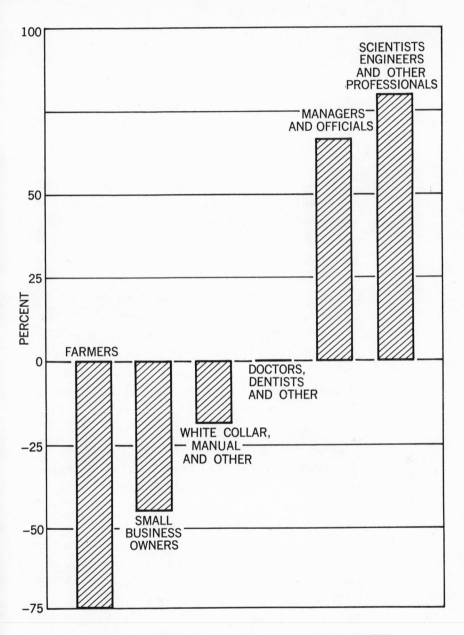

INCOME STATUS OF THE TECHNICAL ELITE,
1950-1960 CHANGE

151

CHART 17

HIGH INCOME PROFESSIONALS AND MANAGERS, % GAIN 1950-1960

Census tabulations of high-income professionals and managers show that scientists and engineers scored by far the greatest relative gains between 1950 and 1960, along with those scored by salaried managers. Unlike the preceding charts which referred to household income, the data below relate to total income of individuals reporting themselves to the Census as professionals or managers earning over $7,000 in 1950, and over $10,000 in 1960. It may be noted that the totality of such high income managers and professionals can be taken as a working definition of what constitutes modern "management," since they account for the operation and direction of the bulk of corporate enterprise today.

Those earning over $7,000 represented the top 3.5 of persons with income in 1950. Of 1,189,000 professionals and managers reporting incomes of over $7,000 in 1950 there were 13,000 natural scientists, 77,000 engineers, 349,000 other professionals, 314,000 salaried managers, and 437,000 other (mainly self-employed) managers. In 1960, persons earning over $10,000 represented the top 5% of all income earners. Of the 2,121,000 such persons reporting themselves as professionals or managers, 29,000 were natural scientists, 238,000 were engineers, 670,000 were other types of professionals (including statisticians, actuaries and

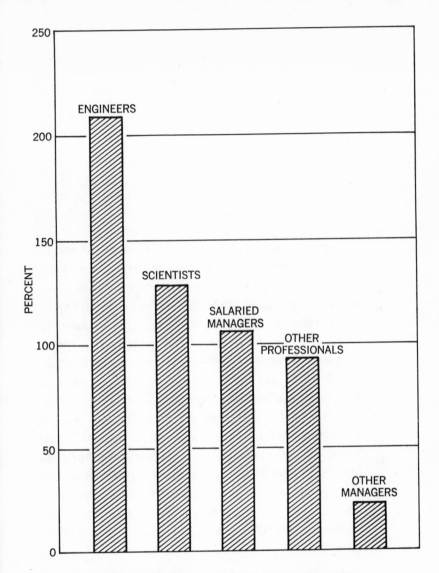

HIGH INCOME PROFESSIONALS AND
MANAGERS, % GAIN 1950-1960

data processing systems people), 648,000 were salaried managers, and 536,000 were other kinds of man-
agers(i.e., mainly self-employed).

Chart 18

HIGH INCOME PROFESSIONALS AND MANAGERS IN MANUFACTURING 1950-1960

A similar process of "professionalization of management" has affected manufacturing particularly. Here the corresponding Census data on high salaried managers and professionals reflect some of the difficulty encountered by scientists and engineers in deciding whether to report as scientists or engineers, or as salaried managers or under other occupational titles. Thus, where the 1960 Census reported a total of 541,000 scientists and engineers in manufacturing, the National Science Foundation post-censal survey has determined that there were an additional 73,000 scientists and engineers in manufacturing, but who reported themselves under other professional and managerial occupations. Estimates of high-income professionals and managers in manufacturing geared to the conservative Census totals are given in thousands below:

	1950 (All earning over $7,000)	1960 (All earning over $10,000)	% Gain 1950-1960
Engineers	43	175	307
Scientists	7	18	157
Other professionals	52	125	140
Salaried Managers, N.E.C.	120	261	118
Other Managers	76	80	5
Total	298	659	121

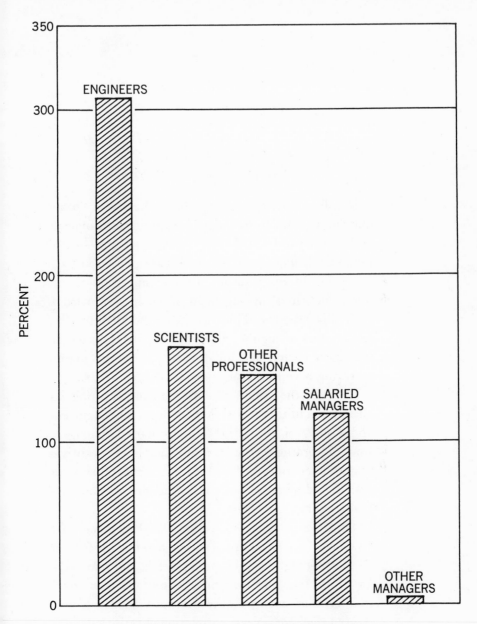

HIGH INCOME PROFESSIONALS AND
MANAGERS IN MANUFACTURING
1950-1960

155

CHART 19

THE CHANGING COMPOSITION OF CORPORATE MANAGEMENT IN MANUFACTURING 1950-1960

It will be noted in the preceding chart that "other managers" (mainly self-employed managers, officials and proprietors) was the only managerial-professional group that made virtually no advance between 1950 and 1960. In any measure of the composition of *corporate* industrial management, it would seem wise to omit this category. Thus, in the period 1950 to 1960 the number of highly paid professionals and salaried managers responsible for directing corporate manufacturing activities rose from 222,000 to 579,000.

In 1960, the technical elite in manufacturing included in addition to 193,000 scientists and engineers, about 60% of the 261,000 high-salaried managers, since, according to the Harvard sample of executives in manufacturing, 45% in 1961 had technical training and 15% discharged technical functions without formal training (see Chart 8).

Thus, for 1960, there were 350,000 members of a technical elite in manufacturing making up 60% of all 579,000 high-salaried professionals and managers. In 1950, the corresponding percentage was much smaller. For example, the Harvard Study demonstrated the high inverse correlation of technical training to age (Chart 10). Thus while 45% of all managers in 1961 had technical training, the corre-

156

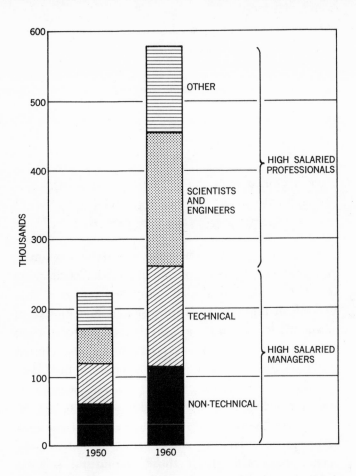

THE CHANGING COMPOSITION OF CORPORATE
MANAGEMENT IN MANUFACTURING 1950-1960

---

sponding percentage in 1950 as suggested by this age distribution would be about 35. Making allowance for those managers discharging technical functions without training, it appears likely that no more than half of the 120,000 salaried managers in 1950 were technical; consequently in 1950, the technical elite in manufacturing probably numbered less than 110,000 persons.

157

CHART 20

THE TECHNICAL ELITE AS A COMPONENT OF CORPORATE MANAGEMENT IN MANUFACTURING, 1950-1965

The technical domination of corporate management in manufacturing occurred in the 1950-1960 decade. In 1950, the technical elite comprised no more than 50% of all high-salaried professionals and managers in manufacturing, but by 1960 the percentage rose to 60%. It must be remembered that these Census-based estimates are extremely conservative, since no allowance is made here, for example, for mathematicians and data-processing experts who choose to report themselves to the Census as auditors, statisticians, or actuaries, considered by the Census to be professional occupations other than those of natural science. Similarly, scientists and engineers increasingly choose to report themselves as editors, authors, teachers, or as nonsalaried managers, and thus escape enumeration as part of our technical elite, as the National Science Foundation discovered in its post-Censal survey of scientists and engineers in manufacturing. Nevertheless, so rapid is the pace of "technicalization" of salaried management indicated here, that by 1965 nearly two out of every three high-salaried professionals and managers in manufacturing can be confidently counted as members of the new technical elite.

158

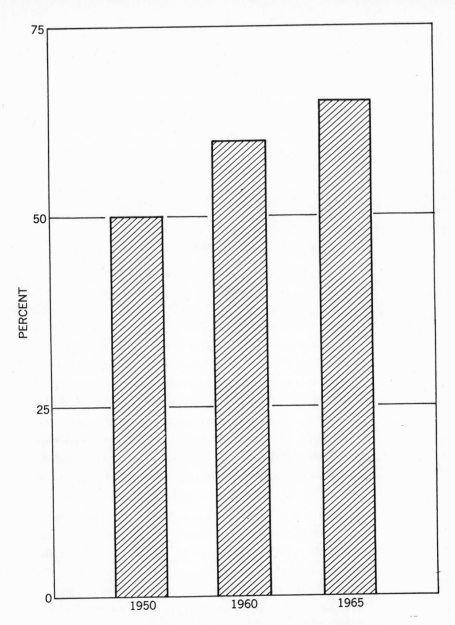

THE TECHNICAL ELITE AS A COMPONENT
OF CORPORATE MANAGEMENT IN
MANUFACTURING, 1950-1965

159

CHART 21

OCCUPATIONS OF FATHERS OF BIG BUSINESS EXECUTIVES

The charts shown in this section are taken from *The Big Business Executive/1964,* published by Scientific American (New York, 1965). They represent the principal findings of a survey of the social and cultural backgrounds of approximately 1,000 of the top officers (president and chairman or principal vice president) of the 600 largest U.S. non-financial corporations. The study, sponsored by Scientific American, was conducted by Market Statistics Inc., of New York City, in collaboration with Dr. Mabel Newcomer and was undertaken to update Dr. Newcomer's study, The Big Business Executive — The Factors That Made Him: 1900-1950 (New York: Columbia University Press).

In this chart it is clear that top executives in industry have been coming in increasing numbers from families headed by employees and professional men (especially engineers) rather than businessmen and company heads.

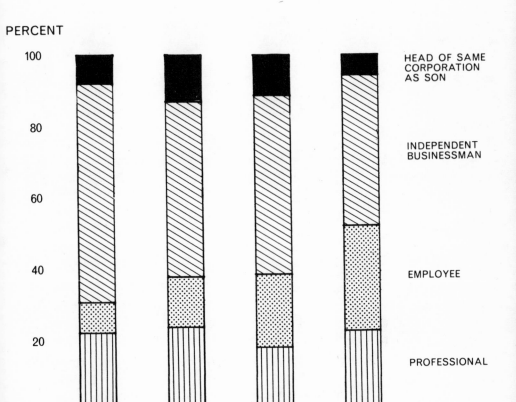

PERCENT

100

80

60

40

20

0

1900   1925   1950   1964

HEAD OF SAME
CORPORATION
AS SON

INDEPENDENT
BUSINESSMAN

EMPLOYEE

PROFESSIONAL

OCCUPATIONS OF FATHERS OF
BIG BUSINESS EXECUTIVES

161

Chart 22

EDUCATION OF BIG BUSINESS EXECUTIVES

A significant index of the professionalization of the big business executive is the doubling of the percentage with some higher education between 1900 (just under 40 percent) and 1964 (more than 90 percent). The percentages with college degrees and graduate training among younger executives consistently exceeded the corresponding percentages among older executives in each year studied after 1900.

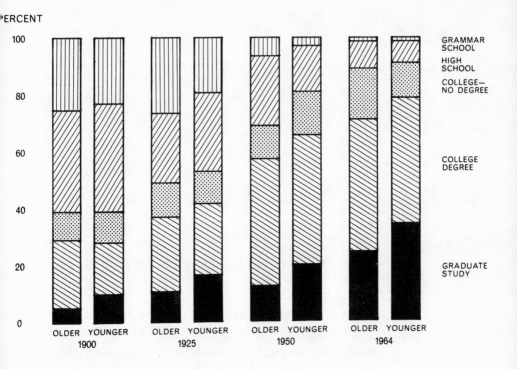

PERCENT

100 — GRAMMAR SCHOOL
      HIGH SCHOOL
      COLLEGE— NO DEGREE

80

60 — COLLEGE DEGREE

40

20 — GRADUATE STUDY

0

OLDER YOUNGER   OLDER YOUNGER   OLDER YOUNGER   OLDER YOUNGER
      1900   1925   1950   1964

EDUCATION OF BIG BUSINESS EXECUTIVES

163

Chart 23

EDUCATION OF BIG BUSINESS EXECUTIVES
1964

The educational attainments of the big business executives as of the year 1964 are charted here in detail. To the total with technical background this chart suggests the addition of the executives (5 percent) who acquired their technical training on the job or brought special gifts for invention and innovation to their organizations. In a number of notable cases, in recent years, such men have been the founders or principal organizers of their firms.

PERCENT

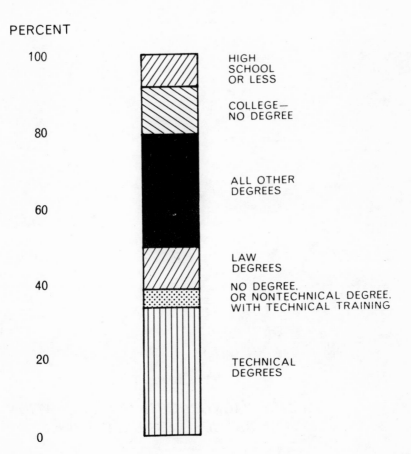

100 — HIGH SCHOOL OR LESS

COLLEGE— NO DEGREE

80

ALL OTHER DEGREES

60

LAW DEGREES

40 — NO DEGREE. OR NONTECHNICAL DEGREE. WITH TECHNICAL TRAINING

20 — TECHNICAL DEGREES

0

EDUCATION OF BIG BUSINESS EXECUTIVES
1964

CHART 24

*FAMILY BACKGROUND AND EDUCATION
OF BIG BUSINESS EXECUTIVES*

In 1964, the percentage of executives from poor
homes who were qualified by undergraduate degrees
and by graduate study was just about equal to corresponding percentages for executives from wealthy
homes. This contrasts sharply with the situation in
1900 shown by the bar graphs at left.

166

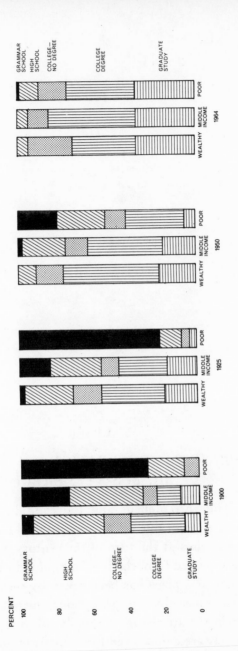

FAMILY BACKGROUND AND EDUCATION
OF BIG BUSINESS EXECUTIVES

167

CHART 25

PRINCIPAL OCCUPATIONAL EXPERIENCE OF BIG BUSINESS EXECUTIVES

The entrepreneur and the capitalist who played such a major role in the organizing of large corporate enterprises at the turn of the century has practically disappeared from the top ranks of industrial management. His place has been taken by the career executive, especially by professional men among whom engineers are the most rapidly growing group. These trends are emphasized by comparison of the occupational experience of the older and younger men in each of the study years.

168

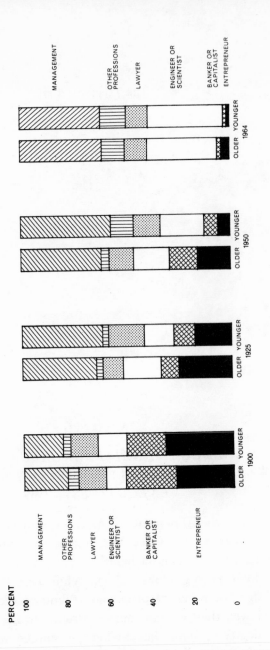

PERCENT

100 — MANAGEMENT

80 — OTHER PROFESSIONS

60 — LAWYER

— ENGINEER OR SCIENTIST

40 — BANKER OR CAPITALIST

20

— ENTREPRENEUR

0

MANAGEMENT

OTHER PROFESSIONS

LAWYER

ENGINEER OR SCIENTIST

BANKER OR CAPITALIST

ENTREPRENEUR

OLDER YOUNGER
1900

OLDER YOUNGER
1925

OLDER YOUNGER
1950

OLDER YOUNGER
1964

PRINCIPAL OCCUPATIONAL EXPERIENCE
OF BIG BUSINESS EXECUTIVES

CHART 26

EDUCATIONAL BACKGROUND OF
TECHNICAL AND NONTECHNICAL
EXECUTIVES — 1964

Nearly 90 percent of the top executives who were educated in science and engineering are formally qualified by the bachelor's degree; about 30 percent went on to graduate school. While a smaller percentage (65 percent) of the nontechnical executives followed their college courses through to the bachelor's degree a somewhat higher percentage went on to graduate school and graduate degrees, principally in law.

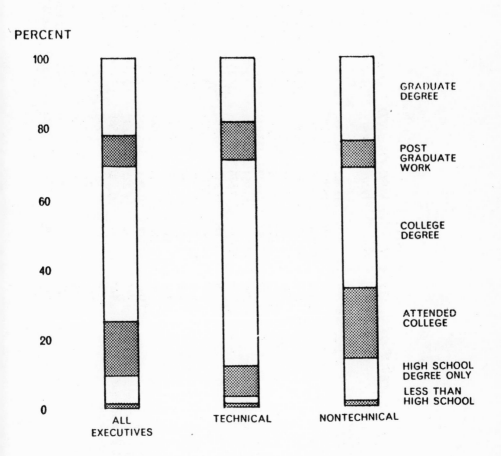

PERCENT

100

80

60

40

20

0

ALL
EXECUTIVES

TECHNICAL

NONTECHNICAL

GRADUATE
DEGREE

POST
GRADUATE
WORK

COLLEGE
DEGREE

ATTENDED
COLLEGE

HIGH SCHOOL
DEGREE ONLY

LESS THAN
HIGH SCHOOL

EDUCATIONAL BACKGROUND OF TECHNICAL
AND NONTECHNICAL EXECUTIVES — 1964

APPENDIX

GROWTH IN THE NUMBER OF NATURAL SCIENTISTS AND ENGINEERS 1900-1960

	1900	1910	1920	1930	1940	1950	1960
ALL SCIENTISTS AND ENGINEERS—TOTAL	62,601	129,963	215,865	349,852	485,803	744,021	1,157,100
Teaching	5,086	11,869	18,868	30,797	46,753	78,715	125,100
Nonteaching	57,515	118,094	196,997	319,055	439,050	665,306	1,032,000
ENGINEERS	45,026	92,133	142,238	236,804	336,345	514,728	836,500
Teaching	787	1,678	2,917	6,014	11,545	20,488	27,500
Nonteaching	44,239	90,455	139,321	230,790	324,800	494,240	809,000
SCIENTISTS	17,575	37,830	73,627	113,048	149,458	229,293	320,600
Teaching	4,299	10,191	15,951	24,783	35,208	58,227	97,600
Nonteaching	13,276	27,639	57,676	88,265	114,250	171,066	223,000
CHEMISTS	9,730	17,513	34,448	49,762	63,162	89,000	103,500
Teaching	883	1,240	1,507	2,224	3,157	6,500	11,600
Nonteaching	8,847	16,273	32,941	47,538	60,005	82,500	91,900
PHYSICISTS	400	974	1,875	4,087	6,159	18,073	29,900
Teaching	340	554	739	1,127	1,449	5,273	8,700
Nonteaching	60	420	1,136	2,960	4,710	12,800	21,200
MATHEMATICIANS	1,099	1,787	2,961	5,376	6,825	13,552	31,400
Teaching—Total	545	952	1,225	1,839	2,366	6,350	13,400
Teaching Mathematicians	470	855	1,040	1,581	2,011	5,560	12,000
Teaching Statisticians	75	97	185	258	355	790	1,400
Nonteaching—Total	554	835	1,736	3,537	4,459	7,202	18,000
Mathematicians	18	35	300	645	925	1,700	7,700
Actuaries	125	270	415	550	700	1,150	2,200
Statisticians	411	530	1,021	2,342	2,834	4,352	8,100

GROWTH IN THE NUMBER OF NATURAL SCIENTISTS AND ENGINEERS 1900-1960
(Continued)

	1900	1910	1920	1930	1940	1950	1960
BIOLOGISTS	2,146	3,660	8,893	12,620	16,984	22,266	40,700
Teaching	1,146	1,751	2,285	3,872	6,051	9,466	21,500
Nonteaching	1,000	1,909	6,608	8,748	10,933	12,800	19,200
EARTH SCIENTISTS	400	801	1,186	3,324	5,484	13,393	23,200
Teaching	160	401	486	824	1,184	1,893	3,700
Nonteaching	240	400	700	2,500	4,300	11,500	19,500
AGRICULTURAL SCIENTISTS	1,000	2,110	4,996	10,328	15,010	28,892	39,500
Teaching	150	364	826	2,060	4,210	8,000	14,000
Nonteaching	850	1,746	4,170	8,268	10,800	20,892	25,500
MEDICAL AND OTHER SCIENTISTS	2,800	10,985	19,268	27,551	35,834	44,117	52,400
Teaching	1,075	4,929	8,883	12,837	16,791	20,745	24,700
Nonteaching	1,725	6,056	10,385	14,714	19,043	23,372	27,700

NOTE: Decennial census reports, from which the above data for nonteaching chemists and engineers are taken, first began the separate enumeration of other natural scientists in 1950. However, since some scientists and engineers might sometimes report themselves to the Census Bureau as teachers, physicians, or managers or officials, in recent years the National Science Foundation has maintained independent and more complete rosters of the universe of scientists and engineers in the U.S. The 1960 estimates above are accordingly taken from the NSF tabulation *Scientists, Engineers, and Technicians in the 1960's* (NSF 63-34), p. 34.

Backward extrapolations from 1960 to 1900 were made separately for scientists and engineers engaged in college and university teaching and those employed in industry and government. The estimates of teaching scientists and engineers were derived from Dael Wolfle's *America's Resources of Specialized Talent*, Harper Bros., 1954, pp. 119, 125 and 292. For each field, it was assumed that the total engaged in teaching and nonteaching positions would, in the period 1900 to 1960, move in rough conformance with the total membership recorded in major national technical societies covering that field. The conformance can only be rough because of the unknown degree of duplication in membership rolls, and the uncertain degree of coverage attained for any given field.

Societies whose historical membership records were available are listed on the following page (with the 1960 membership total in parentheses). It was not possible to find any society membership records to permit tracing the growth of medical and "other" scientists; they were assumed to follow the trend of all scientists and engineers. Metallurgists were included with engineers, to accord with Census usage prior to 1940.

173

TECHNICAL SOCIETIES

PHYSICS
    American Physical Society (16,099)
    American Association of Physics Teachers (5,032)
    Optical Society of America (2,560)
    Acoustical Society of America (2,782)
    Society of Rheology (564)

MATHEMATICS
    American Mathematical Society (6,725)
    Mathematical Association of America (9,254)
    American Statistical Association (7,515)
    Society for Industrial and Applied Mathematics (1,543)
    American Society of Actuaries (2,000)
    Casualty Actuarial Society (360)

BIOLOGY
    American Society of Naturalists (651)
    American Association of Anatomists (1,313)
    American Phytopathological Society (2,155)
    American Physiological Society (2,134)
    Botanical Society of America (2,276)
    Mycological Society of America (792)
    American Society for Microbiology (6,365)
    Society for Protozoologists (677)
    American Bryological Society (205)
    American Society of Ichthyologists and Herpetologists
        (1,086)

AGRICULTURAL SCIENCE
    American Society for Horticultural Science (2,375)
    American Society for Agronomy (4,246)
    American Society of Plant Taxonomists (525)

EARTH SCIENCE
    American Geophysical Union (6,219)
    Association of Engineering Geologists (189)
    American Institute of Mining, Metallurgical and
        Petroleum Engineers (34,852)
    Geological Society of America (6,000)

174

INDEX

INDEX

176

177